I'm Not Prepared to
Accept That!

Philip Whitmarsh

I'm Not Prepared to Accept That!
My Tussle with Polio

To Bill

many thanks for your
interest & support

Phil
5/4/2008

AKEMAN PRESS

Published by Akeman Press, 58 Minster Way, Bath BA2 6RL
www.akemanpress.com

Copyright © Philip Whitmarsh 2008

ISBN: 978-0-9546138-8-4

Printed by Short Run Press, Exeter

To Christine, Kevin and Justin

CONTENTS

ACKNOWLEDGEMENTS

This is probably the most difficult part of the book to write because so many people have helped me since my story appeared on television in February 2007. I want to thank all of you – without your help and encouragement I could not have done it. Please forgive me if I have not mentioned you by name but this is a real challenge as there are so many of you. I include many friends old and new, especially Rotarians, schoolmates, and fellow councillors. Special thanks go to Dave and Jan Norton, Derek Taylor, John Moxon, John Hyde, Molly Butler and Marion Barnes.

Thanks also to Testimony Films of Bristol who made the documentary broadcast on ITV West; Marie Carter, Health Sciences Librarian at the Francis Costello Library, Robert Jones & Agnes Hunt Orthopaedic Hospital Trust near Oswestry; Elizabeth Boardman, Archivist at the Oxfordshire Health Archives; Tina Craig, Deputy Head of Library & Information Services at the Royal College of Surgeons; and Colin Johnston, archivist at the Bath Record Office.

Thanks to the Western Daily Press, and to the Frome Times and the Somerset Standard for permission to quote from articles published during my mayoral year.

Thanks to David Heath, MP, his wife Caz and PA Claire Hudson for the photograph on page 157; to Phil Bishop for the official mayoral photograph on page 227; to Mark Johnston of Wellington, Somerset for the photograph on page 213; and to Deborah Gray of the Journal of Bone and Joint Surgery for permission to reproduce the photograph of Miss Forrester-Brown on page 221, which is the copyright © of the British Editorial Society of Bone and Joint Surgery.

Thanks also to my patient publishers, Andrew and Kirsten; to Les White, Bob Giddings and Ted Honderich, who inspired me to believe I had an interesting story to tell; and a special thanks to my wife, Christine, and my two sons, Kevin and Justin, who have given me so much encouragement, together with my sister, Margaret, who also supplied many of the early family photographs from my Mum's photograph album. You always told me I could do it – I hope you are right.

Philip Whitmarsh,
Frome, March 2008

FOREWORD
by David Heath, MP

There are some people who seem to embody a place and a time. Phil Whitmarsh is one of those people. For me, and for many others, Phil is, simply, Old Frome (and he won't thank me for stressing the 'old' bit!). If anyone personifies the spirit of the town, or at least the town as it was, it is Phil, and although times change, as his book eloquently sets out, Frome has managed to change with them. And I can entirely identify with him when he describes taking umbrage at the ultimate insult for any man of Somerset – being accused of coming from Wiltshire!

Writing as he does of his experiences, from the 'dunces' class' as he describes it (and Phil is certainly no dunce), to coping with bullying in an age when it was just as hurtful as it is recognised as being today, to his period as Mayor of the town, you get a real sense not only of the man himself but the evolution of Frome. The town has changed from being a Somerset market town, agricultural and a little bit rough at the edges (growing up in Wells, Frome was always considered a bit of a poor relation), to a thriving place which retains its character but embraces change, and which has become the subject of endless articles from London scribblers who wish to share their 'discovery'.

There are many people in Frome who have sought Phil's advice over the years, whether professionally or in his role as a councillor. It's been good advice. This book sets out a personal journey, and gives real insights into both his family and the community he was born into, grew up in, and served.

Thanks, Phil, for setting it all down. It's a treat to read.

David Heath CBE,
Member of Parliament for Somerton and Frome

PREFACE

by Robert Giddings

I have the great pleasure of knowing Phil Whitmarsh. We are both Somerset lads and we both share the experience of boyhood polio in the good old days when it was by no means rare. We both featured in the recent television film A West Country Childhood: Reaching for Dreams. So I must here confess a personal interest.

This is a fine book that tells a great story. It is a story that needs telling over and over again. Because what Phil has to say is always true.

Handicap, disability, being crippled -- whatever you care to call it – is a social matter as well as a personal thing. Phil was, and is, a brave person. He had a dreadful illness early as a young boy. He has endured and triumphed over its lasting effects to go on to lead a successful, happy and fulfilled life. Nothing can diminish the considerable nature of that achievement.

But, as he recounts in this splendid book, it is not simply a matter of personal bravery overcoming immense odds. It is a collective achievement involving friends, teachers, medical and institutional help.

And this is my gripe with Political Correctness. It is not what they call you that matters – it's how they treat you. Phil learned this very early in his life and he learned how to deal with it. His treatment of the school bully sets the tone for the whole story. But he also learned and describes so well here, that it's not just a matter of single combat.

Disability is as much socially as physically defined. Phil has learned and experienced this and his lively, straight-from-the-shoulder narrative tells a story that's impressive, moving, frequently funny and always relevant.

This is not just a book for the 'physically challenged' or carers or friends or relatives of someone who is handicapped – this is a great human story with much to teach us all. You'll be touched by this book and it will make you laugh. But you will take something from it you'll never forget.

'Am I not a man and a brother?' Shakespeare asks. You are. We are all brothers and sisters. And the sooner we act like it, the better.

Robert Giddings
January 2008

PROLOGUE

Poliomyelitis

Poliomyelitis comes from two Greek words – 'polio' meaning grey and 'myelon' which refers to the spinal column. The disease, generally referred to as polio or infantile paralysis, attacks the spinal column resulting in paralysis. It is a notifiable and highly infectious viral disease caused by three types of poliovirus, with symptoms similar to flu – sore throat, headache, fever, vomiting, stiffness of the back and neck, and abdominal pains. Anyone infected with the virus can remain infectious for up to 16 weeks, hence the need for isolation in treating the disease.

In severe cases the central nervous system is attacked, causing varying degrees of paralysis. The parts of the body most likely to be affected are the arms and especially the legs. Many survivors are so badly paralysed that they become totally immobile and are confined to wheelchairs. In extreme cases, where the muscles that control breathing, swallowing or the heart are also affected, death may result. Approximately 1% of those infected by the poliovirus develop paralysis. Of these, 50% make a full recovery, 25% continue to suffer mild paralysis and 25% severe paralysis.

The disease was once common and there were many epidemics until the early 1960s, particularly in hot weather. Families lived in fear of an outbreak every summer. Today, however, it has been virtually eliminated worldwide. The introduction of the Salk vaccine in 1955 and the Sabin oral vaccine in 1963 resulted in massive reductions in new cases of the disease. In 1955 there were around 6,000 cases in the UK alone: the last case notified in Europe, however, occurred in Turkey in 1998. In 2003 the World Health Organization officially declared that polio had been eradicated in Europe. The modern polio vaccine (IPV) used since 2004 is given in a programme of around five injections, the first at between two to four months and the last in the teens.

Although polio can be successfully prevented by vaccination, the virus, once contracted, cannot be treated with drugs. If you were born before 1962, it is recommended that you take medical advice on vaccination, as you may not be fully immune (you require immunity from three types of virus), even if you have had polio.

Some former polio victims have experienced problems in later life, such as muscle or joint pain, loss of muscle bulk, sleep disturbance, intolerance of the cold, breathing and/or swallowing difficulties, etc. These are grouped together under the heading of Post Polio Syndrome (PPS), a condition which is now widely recognised, with help, advice and support all available.

Some famous people who have suffered polio include Franklin D Roosevelt, John Thaw, Jack Nicklaus, Donovan and Ian Dury.

A useful contact is: The Polio Fellowship, Eagle Office Centre, The Runway, South Ruislip, Middlesex, HA4 6SE – Freephone 0800 0180586 – *info@britishpolio.org.uk* – *www.britishpolio.org.uk*

CHAPTER ONE

The Fall

It is Monday 25 June 1945. The sun is shining and I'm happily playing in the garden with my brother Brian and my sister Margaret. I am four years old, Brian is seven and Margaret is three.

We have just recovered from a serious bout of measles. All three of us were in bed for several days. The family doctor, Dr Walker, attended us regularly because he was so concerned. Margaret was particularly poorly as her spots wouldn't form properly. They appeared to be under her skin. Brian and I, however, had an impressive amount of spots all over our bodies. We tried to count them most days, but there were so many we were forced to give up.

Margaret had become infected after us, mainly because she wouldn't leave us alone when we were ill, often helping mum bring food and drink up to our bedroom. She was afraid of Dr Walker and used to hide behind the bed when he visited. She slid off the bed and out of sight as soon as he entered the bedroom, occasionally peeping over the edge of the bed but quickly disappearing again if anyone looked in her direction. He found this amusing and joked about this with mum, giving a nod and a wink. They pretended not to have noticed her.

Most of the time we were in bed the curtains were drawn, as bright light was unbearable. When we were allowed up for the first time we were very weak and unsteady on our feet. We had certainly suffered badly.

Now all that is behind us as we play in the midsummer sunshine. Gosh, it is good to be playing out in the fresh air after being confined to bed for so long. The air buzzes and murmurs with joy and happiness and I am back to my old active – and mischievous – self again.

We live at 80 The Butts at Frome in Somerset, a large old stone house which we rent from Mr Smart. Part of the house is divided off to form a lock-up fish and chip shop run by a Mr Brimson.

My first portrait – aged 18 months

I was born here on 30 October 1940. My sister followed less than two years later on 26 April 1942. Brian, the oldest, had been born in a nursing home at Trowbridge in Wiltshire on 11 March 1938. My sister and I were born downstairs in the 'best room' at the front of the house, which was converted to a delivery room for the purpose. With the war in full swing, it was probably considered safer than the bedrooms upstairs.

Even though I wasn't yet two, I can remember my sister being born. It is my earliest memory. Her birth coincided with the bombing of Bath, which took place over two nights – 25 and 26 April 1942. I can remember everyone standing looking out of the window as flashes lit up the sky, followed by muffled bangs, and commenting on how close they seemed. Even at that age, I could feel the tenseness and fear as the bombardment dragged on. It was certainly a time to remember – my sister's birth made it doubly memorable!

Our garden is enormous, with two lawns, vegetable plots, a plum orchard and an allotment used by my uncle. My parents also keep pigs, chickens, rabbits and ducks. The pigs are sold at the local market, along with the eggs laid by the chickens and ducks. A few are kept back for us, of course. If we're lucky we sometimes have a rabbit for dinner as well.

I loved my tricycle – the photo above gives an idea how big our garden was – the large building in the background was the Whitewell Boys' Home. Below is an another photo of me on my tricycle, hitched up to Brian's car with the woodpile in the background.

At one end of the garden is a huge woodpile made up of large branches and tree trunks. It belongs to a local fuel merchant, who cuts it up into logs for his customers. Apart from the rent

3

Above: me, Margaret and Brian on the woodpile; below, one of my favourite photos, showing that I did once have two good legs and loved a ride with driver Brian

Above, my favourite photo of my early childhood, pointing something out to Margaret and Brian; below, Dad gives Margaret and me a lift

he pays for the site, this means we have an endless supply of firewood – and a great place to go on climbing expeditions with our friends. It's also a terrific place to hide when we play hide and seek.

Dad also rents out a massive hangar-like building, known as the Big Black Shed. The potato-peeling machine for the fish and chip shop is kept there, as well as the fuel merchant's saw bench, operated by a small petrol engine and belt drive. A couple of our neighbours also use part of the shed as a store.

Dad is away in London, driving a lorry for a local builder who has a contract to repair or demolish houses. We haven't seen him for weeks. Mum worries about him but says very little to us. He works very hard and his job is dangerous. Sometimes the houses he pulls down are still on fire! My brother and I miss him very much, although my sister, who has only just turned three, doesn't seem to know who he is. I like the muscles on my dad's arms – he makes them hard to see if I can press them in.

We are so lucky to have such a wonderful garden to play in.

5

Above, kings of the castle on top of the woodpile, from the left, Margaret, David Daniels, Jean Daniels, me, Ray Daniels and Brian; below, Anthony Ames from next door with me, Brian and Margaret round the tin bath

Many of our friends come to play here as well because we have so much room. It's so much more fun than the local park.

Today we've brought a tin bath out and are playing with jugs and a wooden boat carved from a scrap of wood by my grandfather. It's great fun as we splash about happily in the water. No arguments either!

A friend from a few doors away arrives. We decide to go and play a different game on the top lawn. Although my friend seems keen on the water sports, four children around a small bath seems a bit crowded. And, as well as wanting a change, we're somewhat damp by now and need to dry off!

We decide to play piggyback. Brian volunteers to carry us around the lawn on his back. Good old Bry! Margaret has first go because she's the youngest. My turn's next. Brian carries me around the lawn once, but I want another go. Brian tells me to let my friend have a turn. Playfully I struggle. Brian shrugs me off. I lose my grip and fall to the ground.

I don't fall heavily enough to hurt myself, but as I go to stand up my legs don't seem to want to work. I don't understand what's happening. Brian realises something's wrong and runs into the house shouting, 'mum, mum, come quick our Philip's hurt'. She comes running out and tries to help me to my feet. I cannot stand! We have two or three tries but still it's no good. Softly she asks me if I'm playing up. I assure her I'm not! She gently gathers me up, carries me indoors and places me in a big easy chair. She assures me that I'll be all right in a moment.

A few hours later an emergency appointment is made to see Dr Walker at his home. Mother wheels me there in an old pram – the one that has served Brian, Margaret and me so well in the past. It is rather shabby and worn out but it serves the purpose.

On arrival we are shown into the consultation room. I am placed on the couch and the doctor comes in to examine me. He lifts my legs and gently lets them go. They flop back to the couch. Then he produces his stethoscope. I wriggle because it is so cold on my back and chest. The examination continues for several minutes, with the doctor giving the occasional 'hmm' and glancing anxiously towards mum.

He then takes an instrument like a hammer and taps my legs, knees, ankles and arms. There are no reflex actions in my legs, although my arms respond normally. Dr Walker shakes his head, walks over to mum and talks to her in a low voice. For the first time I realise that something is seriously wrong. I have no idea what, but it's obvious that things are far from well.

We return home. On the way mum explains that over the next few days we will have to see if I recover the use of my legs. I will have to try hard to walk if at all possible. If not I will have to go into hospital. 'What is Hospital?' I ask. I know where the building is, but not what happens there. 'It's where you go to get better', she explains. I recall that some years earlier, when learning to speak, I couldn't say 'hospital'. Little did I know then that Frome Victoria Hospital would soon play a major role in my life.

I do little for the rest of the day. I rest in the easy chair. As I feel cold I'm wrapped in a lovely warm grey blanket. I try to stand a couple of times and fall flat on my face. I am not deterred and keep trying again and again – still I just fall over. My legs crumple as soon as they try to take my weight. I am offered some lovely hot toast and a warm milky drink – I just pick and chew it around and around not wanting it. I take a sip of my drink and screw my face up. Mum smiles kindly, takes me in her arms and whispers, 'bed for you, my son'.

Gently she carries me from the living room and upstairs to the bedroom I share with Brian. She places me in bed and tucks me in. I like the way mum tucks me in – this time it seems even nicer. What a lovely mum I have! She then says, 'have some sleep – in the morning perhaps you will feel better'. I feel so calm and comforted, I turn over and drift off into a pleasant restful sleep – most unusual as I'm not usually a good sleeper. Mum and dad always have to creep about if I am asleep, as I'm likely to wake at the least noise –

What a lovely mum!

so different to my brother and sister, who seem to be able to sleep anywhere. But tonight I have no trouble sleeping.

Morning arrives. Mum stands quietly at my bedside and calls 'Philip' to awaken me. Brian is already up. I stir and sit up. I try to slide my legs out of bed. No, they will not move. Mum helps me up. 'Let's try again', she says. Still my legs will not carry me, even with assistance from mum. She sighs and picks me up to carry me downstairs for some breakfast.

I'm not really hungry and after messing with a boiled egg and toasted soldiers I'm placed in the easy chair. I play a few games of flips with Brian and Margaret. This a game where you flip a cigarette card towards a wall until you and your opponent have used up all your cards. The card nearest the wall is the winning throw and the winner collects all the cards. I play this several times and win a game. I try to stand up to collect the cards and fall flat on my face.

Brian and Margaret then go outside to play in the fresh air as mum says this will do them good. She reads me a short story and then starts to prepare dinner. I continue to play flips alone – I have discovered I can crawl on my stomach to collect them. Dad is still away in London working on bomb-damaged buildings. He is trying to get time off to come home, but there seems to be a problem. It doesn't help that the only way mum and dad can communicate with each other is by telegram.

Despite not feeling hungry, I manage to eat a little roast dinner, followed by custard. Then I have a rest and go to sleep.

Brian as a toddler in the pram that was later used to ferry me to the surgery and the hospital. The tall girl next to the pram is my cousin Christina

On waking I don't want any tea, so mum carries me up to bed and tucks me in. I feel so snug and comfortable. She sits with me for a while, stroking my head and cheek with the love and affection only a mother can give, as I drift off to sleep. She sighs and says, 'I think it's hospital for you, my lad'.

The next few days follow a similar pattern. I rest, eat a little and play alone. Not that I am really interested in doing very much. I am quite happy to sit quietly, most unlike me. I also try to walk, but with no success. Brian and Margaret are encouraged to play by themselves and allow me to rest. I don't seem to be showing any sign of improvement.

Thursday evening and mum carries me to bed. She sits with me as I slowly fall asleep. I feel reassured as she watches over me.

The morning of Friday 29 June arrives. Mum wakes me earlier than usual and says, 'Dr Walker wants you to go to hospital today so that you can get better and walk again'. I give a half-smile in acknowledgement.

Mum gives me a wash, using a small flannel and a washbasin filled with warm water. She dresses me in some clean pyjamas, explaining that I will probably be in bed in hospital so I may as well have them on now, to save me the trouble of changing into them there.

I have a little porridge and milk for breakfast. I seem to have a better appetite this morning and eat more than I have done for several days.

'Right then', says mum, 'let's take you to the hospital'.

She wraps me up in a warm grey blanket, puts me in the old pram and pushes me off to the hospital. On the way everyone we pass wants to stop and talk. Mum explains that she must hurry as I have an appointment at the hospital.

I accept all this without question. I have complete confidence that everything is being for done for the best to make sure I recover from my mystery illness.

CHAPTER TWO

The Mystery Disease

It is late morning on Friday 29 June 1945 when we arrive at Frome Victoria Hospital, a large stone building with a commemorative stone 'laid by the Hon Mrs Duckworth of Orchardleigh Nov 9 1899'.

I go inside to meet the nurse who takes mum and I through to a bed that has been prepared for me. It is inside the doors in the downstairs ward just off the main corridor, with a large window behind it.

I have not seen a nurse close up before. They have dresses of different colours, black shiny shoes, white aprons and funny white hats. Some of the hats are bigger than others. Men are walking around in full-length white coats with stethoscopes on their collars. I soon discover that they are the doctors, but at this stage hospital is completely new to me.

My mum's diary for 1945 recording my fall on 25 June and my admission to hospital four days later

The Victoria Hospital – I knew where the building was but not what happened there

The nurse helps me into bed, makes me comfortable and asks my mum a few questions. The nurse smiles at me and tells us that we need to wait a few minutes and a doctor will come to see us. We wait. Mum looks anxious. I, though, am quite unconcerned – I trust my mum!

It seems ages before anything happens. I drift off to sleep and wake to see the bed surrounded by nurses and men and women in white coats. Mum is asked to leave – she is asked to go home!

Suddenly I feel alarmed and frightened – what is going to happen? Screens are pulled around the bed. I am alone in a strange bed, in a strange hospital, with lots of people dressed in strange clothes. I do not understand! The bed covers are removed. I am stripped. Nobody speaks to me. Nobody seems bothered how I feel. All these people are just talking to each other, in deep and frantic voices. What are they going to do to me? I am scared and really frightened. I want to hide but there is nowhere to go.

One by one, the doctors pull me around. My legs and arms are lifted and let flop back on the bed. My arms are pulled and tugged. Hammers are produced. I am tapped and prodded all over. Some of the doctors use stethoscopes to sound my chest. Occasionally I am asked to lift an arm or leg. My arms are all right but I still can't move my legs.

The examination continues for ages, and after everyone else has left a kind nurse comforts me. She encourages me by telling me how good and brave I've been. Then she dresses me. The bed is re-made, I am propped up and the screens are removed.

I can now see the whole of the ward. There are lots of beds, all of them occupied by grown men. I am the only child in here! The men in the beds on either side of me are asleep. Everything is very new and scary and I feel very alone. I do not like hospital. I want to go home. I want to run and walk again. I want to be well.

It is now Wednesday 11 July 1945. I have been in Frome Victoria Hospital almost two weeks. I am amazed that the time has passed so quickly. I can only think it did not seem so long because I was really ill.

Every day I have been subjected to the same ritual, the same examinations. Nothing else seemed to be happening and I was not getting any better. I came to accept the prodding and pulling around, though – it didn't really hurt. I just supposed that was what they did in hospitals. But all the time I wondered when I was going to start to get better, when I would be able to start moving my legs, to get up and walk around again.

Today is a bit different, though, for an orthopaedic surgeon from Bath has been asked to take a look at me. I find out later his name is John Bastow. I also find out later that, after taking a look at me, he is absolutely furious, demanding to know what was everyone thinking of, and saying something along the lines of 'the boy has infantile paralysis – he is infectious – he must go into isolation immediately'.

Not for nothing was this known as the 'mystery disease'. I had lain in hospital for almost two weeks and been pulled and prodded around, and no one was any the wiser until a specialist from Bath was called in.

It is not until much later that I find all this out, though, and find out also that Mr Bastow has diagnosed me with poliomyelitis. Not that it would have meant much to me at the time. I just longed for the day when I would be able to walk and play again.

CHAPTER THREE

Isolation

It was late the same afternoon when my mum arrived at the hospital. I had not seen her very often over the past two weeks as visiting times were restricted. I was very pleased to see her.

'We are going for a ride in a car', she announced.

'Why?' I asked excitedly. I had been on a train and a bus a few times, but a car – wow! Few people had cars in those days unless they were posh or wealthy.

Mum explained that the hospital had told her that a car was coming to take me home. We would not have to wait very long, so my belongings had to be packed quickly away so we could take them with us.

'Mummy, I still can't walk', I said as she packed my things up.

'I know', she replied, not looking at me.

A big black car drew up outside the hospital and a man came into the ward to see if we were ready. Mum carried me to the car and the driver carried my belongings.

I felt so good – and going in a car was a real treat! We sat in the back seat, me on mum's lap as she held me close, gently but firmly in her arms. I was going home.

The car moved away and I looked out of the window. I was nice and high up on my mum's lap so I could see really well. Children were playing near the hospital – people were walking along the road – flowers, trees and grass looked brighter than I had ever remembered them. To be out of that hospital and driving along in a car through the summer sunlight seemed incredible. And I was going home!

We had been in the car for about ten minutes when I turned to mum and asked her why it was taking so long. I may have been only four years and nine months old, but I knew we didn't live far from the hospital. We had often walked past it on our way to and from the shops.

'We are going the long way round so that you can have some lovely fresh air, and see the birds and trees – you need it after being in hospital for so long.'

I accepted her explanation without question and turned back to look out of the window.

The car pulled up outside a large building. I knew this wasn't home, but I didn't question it. The driver pointed to a door and mum picked me up and carried me towards it.

She knocked and the door was opened by a large nurse with a big white hat. Before I knew what was happening she had taken me from my mum and whisked me inside. Where my mum went I have no idea.

I was absolutely horrified. I had been misled. I was not going home after all. I was in another hospital surrounded by nurses. I struggled, cried, screamed, shouted and did everything possible to make it clear what I thought of this unfair deceit! Why had mum and everyone else treated me like this?

My mother and father were honest, fair and truthful parents. We children had been encouraged to be the same. Truth was regarded as paramount. I now know that my mum absolutely hated that moment when she handed me over, and the deception she played on me. Many times afterwards, particularly when I was older, she shook her head and said emotionally, 'that was cruel'. Unbeknown to me, she had pleaded with the hospital staff not to mislead me, but to no avail. She only wanted to tell me the truth, that I had to go to a special hospital to get better, but had been overruled.

I was taken to what I later realised was an isolation ward and put to bed. I was absolutely frantic! It is difficult to describe what the room was like, as I have never seen anything like it since. What I remember was that it either had no windows or they were blacked out. It was dimly lit and the door was always closed. I was alone most of the time. Everyone who came into the room wore a mask over their mouth and nose. I didn't see a full face for weeks. I think they also wore white suits or overalls. I can't be sure, but their uniforms were definitely covered up. I was so frightened. I had no idea what was happening and nobody bothered to tell me. I stayed in this dreadful place for several weeks – I have never been able to find out exactly how long – frightened and alone almost the whole time.

I was eventually moved to the small children's ward. What a joy this was! I was in the 'Baby's Ward' in the Bath & Wessex

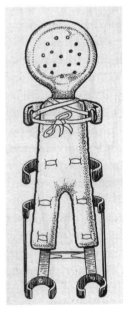

...like a padded ginger-bread man with no arms

Orthopaedic Hospital at Combe Park in Bath. I immediately felt at home. There were around two dozen beds and cots. The children ranged from small babies to boys and girls of five or six. As I was almost five, I was one of the older children on the ward.

Shortly after I arrived I was wheeled into a treatment room. The nurses explained to me that I had to go on a frame to keep my legs still so that they would get better. This frame looked like a padded gingerbread man with no arms but with metal frames for the feet. Both of my legs were bandaged from the ankles to the groin to fix them to the frame. My feet were also bandaged to oblong uprights at the end of each of the padded legs. Flat metal straps were bent over my chest and tied securely so that I could not sit up. Once on the frame I had to lie on my back, unable to move any part of my body apart from my head and arms. Then the frame was raised up from the bed so that bedpans and urine bottles could be slid underneath.

For the first few days, I was so pleased to see activity around me that all this did not bother me that much. I could chat with the boys on either side of me and, as they could both run around, we often played and shared toys. There was so much happening and the nurses were so kind and always smiling. Some of the nicer ones used to kiss me goodnight. I really liked that! It was such a relief being in here after that other horrible place. I also had a soft stuffed toy monkey that was given to me to hold and cuddle up to as I went to sleep at night. So altogether I was quite chirpy again.

Soon I had settled into my new home and I began to get restless and frustrated at having to lie on my back all the time. I was beginning to feel more confident. I wanted to move more than my head and arms. I began to untie the metal straps fixed over my chest. After I untied them I bent them upwards so that I could sit up. The nurses soon caught me and their attitude changed from happy and smiley to angry and cross. Immediately I was tied down again, and this time the straps seemed tighter than ever. Undeterred, I soon undid them again, but this time I was more careful and only sat up when there were no nurses watching. This carried on for some time but each time I eventually got caught. I sometimes think they must have secretly spied on me, as often when I was lying down they would come and inspect the straps. They had become craftier than me!

Eventually one of the metal straps broke because of the continuous bending backwards and forwards. I was certainly in trouble now. The frame had to be taken away for repair, so I had a short respite from my restrictive prison. Gosh, was that good – even though it was short-lived!

The frame returned a few hours later and once again I was strapped to it. The nurses were very cross and the ward sister was called to give me a severe reprimand. I was told firmly that I must never undo my straps again. I never did – but it wasn't for want of trying! While the frame was being repaired, the straps had been fixed in such a way that I was never able to untie them again. I think the ward sister was very shrewd and experienced in such encounters! She knew exactly how to deal with mischievous patients like me.

The months passed uneventfully enough. Mum came to visit me as often as she could, usually about once a fortnight. Visiting was restricted and she had to travel from Frome to Bath, some 14 miles, by bus. I played games and developed friendships with other children in the ward. New children arrived, others left, some of them had to have operations.

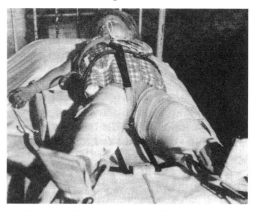

The type of frame I was strapped to for almost ten months

As I was lying on my back all the time, it eventually became very sore and covered in painful boils. I was taken off the frame and laid on my stomach with a firm wedge-shaped pillow to support my chest and keep me in a slightly upward position. It was such a relief to be off the frame and have so much freedom of movement. I could also see much more. My back was very painful, but more painful still were the hot kaolin poultices used to treat it. I had to have it treated and dressed regularly, with the dreadful poultices applied to it until the boils and sores had completely healed up. Still, at least I had said goodbye to the frame!

Now that I was off the frame the remedial treatment started in earnest. I visited the gym frequently, where my legs were exercised and massaged and I was encouraged to move them as much as possible. The parallel walking bars provided support as I tried to learn to walk again. Day by day, week by week, I began to get stronger. It was a slow and tedious process but the staff were tremendous and the encouragement superb.

I was also taken to the baths fed by water from Bath's hot springs a couple of times a week. This was really good! I was placed on my back in a canvas sling and lowered into the water where I had to do various exercises and wriggle and move my legs as much as possible. It was so much easier to move while floating comfortably in the warm water. I became aware that, although my left leg was very weak, my right leg was growing stronger. I had been paralysed from the waist down but recovery was under way.

Christmas 1945 was my first one in hospital. It was a really happy and joyous occasion. The ward was decorated, we all had stockings to hang up and we all received presents. The nurses,

Christmas 1945 – my first in hospital. I'm on the extreme left, held by a nurse. Just look how my socks hang on my almost lifeless legs

sisters, doctors and staff all dressed up and for a few days it was one big party – not like a hospital at all! Another bonus was that Brian and Margaret could visit me – I had not seen them since going into hospital in Frome almost six months earlier. The discipline in hospitals in those days was very strict: parents had limited access and children were not normally allowed to visit at all. It was thought they would upset the children on the ward. There may have been something in this. Child patients often cried when their parents left after visiting. My brother and sister seemed shy, but I put this down to their being afraid of hospitals, having not been in one before. I later discovered they were afraid they might be kept in like me!

My right leg continued to grow stronger, but my left leg showed little sign of improvement and I was fitted with a full-length calliper or leg iron so that I could walk. I was soon on my feet again and that was a fantastic feeling – freedom again! There was a large grey horse on wheels which I used to lean over and propel around the ward at great speed. This was terrific fun. Mind you, my steering was not up to much and I regularly crashed into anything in my way. And, although I was able to build up speed quite nicely, I wasn't so good at stopping! Everyone gave me a wide berth, although I never remember anyone stopping me or suggesting I should not do it. Although nothing was ever said, I think deep down they were delighted at my determination and spirit. I think some of them were secretly amazed at what I could do.

I didn't get on very well with my Grandfather Weaver, mum's dad. Some of the family have suggested it was my spirit that he was wary of, but it may actually have come about as a result of something that happened when he visited the hospital with my mum. My grandmother was with him and she was always so kind and friendly and gave me a big hug. My grandfather, though, was shocked to see me so disabled and in a calliper.

My grandfather lived in a the coal-mining village of Peasedown St John, a few miles outside Bath. He had been a miner all his life, finishing up as a 'safety man', a position of some responsibility.

He always wore a large trilby hat, which he took off when he went indoors. I am not sure how the hat came to be on the hospital floor, but when I saw it there I seized the opportunity with relish, setting off around the ward kicking it before me like a football. This was great fun, a brilliant new game, and I kicked it further and further as my excitement mounted.

'Bring that back, it's Gramf's best hat', my mother shouted, but all my grandfather said was, 'let 'en bide!', a North Somerset expression meaning 'leave him alone'.

Gran and Gramf Weaver - complete with trilby - at the seaside

The hat, I believe, survived without suffering any permanent damage, but while it was a wonderful experience – for me – while it lasted, his view of it may have been somewhat different.

A few days later I was discharged. I had been in hospital for ten months. My lack of appetite was still a concern, but I was considered well enough to continue my recovery and improve my walking at home.

CHAPTER FOUR

Recovery

My recovery and rehabilitation continued. I attended weekly physiotherapy sessions, lasting about 30 to 40 minutes, where my leg was massaged. I then had to practice and learn various exercises. These were designed to strengthen the muscles in my left leg, and to improve my posture and keep my back straight. There were many different exercises, which I had to do every morning, after which I lay on my stomach for several hours to rest. By bedtime I would be tired, miserable and exhausted, although this was due to me trying to do too much, particularly playing and running around, rather than too many exercises.

We attended regular outpatient clinics run by Miss Forrester-Brown from the Bath & Wessex Orthopaedic Hospital. These were explosive, demanding, but strangely interesting events. They were held in an old part of Frome, upstairs on the second floor of an old building with a narrow entrance and rickety, winding stairs. As it was an orthopaedic clinic, many of the patients had severe mobility problems, and had great difficulty climbing the stairs. I never heard of anyone being injured by falling, but many parents felt it was dangerous and made sure their children took extra care. This was, of course, before the creation of the National Health Service, so money and facilities were scarce.

Once upstairs we had to go into a small room to undress, irrespective of what was wrong with us. We had to remove all our clothes including our socks. We were then given a fig leaf to wear if we were under 14 and shorts if we were older. Then we put our shoes – without socks – back on. If we were lucky we were also given a flimsy dressing gown that was always too small and covered very little. The room always seemed very cold – I am sure there was no heating – and there we would stand shivering while we waited our turn.

Then we were called into the consultation room and sat on some six or so chairs facing the examination couch in the middle of the room. Yes! Six or so patients at a time watching an examination in progress. No such thing as confidentiality in those days! The pattern of these examinations was always the same. The patient lay on the couch, Miss Forrester-Brown would carry out a thorough inspection and then instruct them to walk up and down, scrutinising them from all angles as they did so. If the patient was not wearing strong supporting shoes, their parents would be strongly rebuked, and if they were wearing sandals a severe lecture about the need for proper shoes followed – it was very humiliating for anyone who didn't have the correct footwear. It also served as a lesson to the waiting band of patients and their parents. During the check-ups, Miss Forrester-Brown dictated at tremendous speed to her secretary, and at the end of each consultation she would give explicit instructions to the parents about what was to be done to help their child's recovery.

My mum found these sessions very embarrassing, especially as Miss Forrester-Brown kept referring to me as 'malnourished' and this was recorded in the notes. My mum was always so calm and reserved, but one day, when Miss Forrester-Brown noted yet again that I was malnourished, she snapped.

'What can I do about it?' she asked, 'he gets the best food and just leaves it'. Even Miss Forrester-Brown was startled at this outburst, as few people dared to stand up to her like that. She replied simply, 'nothing'. Malnourishment was never mentioned again.

The war was over and we played outside more often, but there was still a heavy army presence near Frome. There was an American army base at Marston House, about two miles up the road from our house. When convoys passed us playing in the road outside the fish and chip shop, we cheered excitedly, waved and gave the V for Victory sign. The soldiers often threw sweets and chewing gum to us and smiled as they waved back.

Mum always told us to be careful and not get too friendly with the soldiers and certainly not go anywhere with them, or take a ride in their lorries. We didn't really understand why because we thought they were super guys, but we obeyed all the same. We were

80 The Butts, where I was born and grew up, showing the pavement outside the fish & chip shop that was covered in goodies thrown by American servicemen as they passed the house in a convoy

also warned not to tell them who was or was not living at home, if they asked any questions, but just to come inside, and certainly not bring them to the house. I think we knew there was a good reason to be careful and I don't think we ever disobeyed; we knew they were strangers.

One day as I played with several of my friends, a particularly large convoy passed by, and as we cheered and waved a continuous array of food, sweets, biscuits and chewing gum was thrown from each vehicle as it slowly passed by. The stuff being thrown was non-stop; it just came in a continuous stream. We were soon swamped as the pavement in front of the shop was covered in goodies as the gifts kept on coming.

Once the convoy had gone we all grabbed armfuls of our treats and ran towards our various homes; soon our mums and families joined us and helped to carry it all away. I don't think I had ever seen so much. It was shared out between all our friends and neighbours and was most welcome in those days of shortages and rationing. Mum said later, 'you shouldn't really do that – anyone would think you had not been fed properly – you shouldn't beg', but I remembered it as a red-letter day and was left with the impression that Americans were extremely kind, friendly and generous.

My physical well-being was of prime importance and so I did not return to school but stayed at home to help mum with her chores. We had a smallholding with chickens, pigs, ducks and rabbits which had to be fed every day. Mum did this as dad was driving a lorry for the railway; he had to take an early-morning train to Trowbridge, eight miles away, and did not return home until the evening.

We mixed up the feed for the animals and fed them. I really enjoyed this and mum used to explain why different foodstuffs were needed. I became very proficient at this and often mixed and measured the various items for her. We fed the chickens and ducks with corn and meal blended to make a thick porridge-like mixture. The pigs were fed swill that had been cooked a few days before, usually on a Sunday morning, in a large brick-built boiler; to this was added leftover vegetables and bread scraps from the nearby bakery.

One day when feeding the pigs I asked mum if she remembered when I had tried to milk a pig. She nodded and remarked that it was a stupid and dangerous thing to do and I was lucky they liked children. This had happened before my third birthday. I was with my dad watching a sow with her piglets suckling her.

Above, Dad and my cousin Fred with one of my beloved pigs, with the hen house and plum orchard in the background; below, Brian and I take a ride on the back of a pig under dad's watchful eye

A toddler's-eye view of two of our geese with the pigsty where I tried to milk the pig in the background

'What are they doing?' I asked.

'They are having a drink of milk', my dad replied.

I was used to being around the pigsties and the pigs were used to us children riding on their backs, so a few days later I asked my mum for an empty cocoa tin and took my stool into the pigsty with the sow and piglets. I plonked my stool down beside her, slid the cocoa tin underneath and started pulling at her teats to get some milk. She promptly kicked me out of the pigsty! I was not hurt but my pride was severely dented and I went crying to mum saying, 'the pig won't give me any milk'.

Needless to say I never tried to milk a pig again!

Once all the animals had been fed and cleaned out we collected the freshly-laid eggs, gathered some vegetables from the garden and took them into the house. The eggs were washed and checked to make sure they were undamaged and placed in trays for the egg packers to collect. We kept any that were unsuitable for the packing station. The vegetables were then prepared for dinner. I helped mum to do all this and after lunch rested on my stomach while she read or listened to the radio.

This continued for about a year or so until I was six, when I went back to school. I was behind all the children in my class and could not read or write. I tried hard to read but found it really

difficult. I can't remember much about this time other than going to school in the mornings and resting at home in the afternoons. This continued until I was eight.

My walking continued to improve but there was concern about my left foot which still drooped lifelessly. My physiotherapist tried various exercises and bound it with sticking plaster to hold it in position, but every effort to bring about an improvement had no effect.

Age six, shortly after returning to school

Miss Forrester-Brown decided that I needed an operation to stabilise my foot and fix it in a permanent position with no movement at all, This was referred to as a 'foot block' and entailed shortening the tendons in my foot and fusing the anklebones together. My physiotherapist was not happy about this and tried to persuade mum that I shouldn't have the operation. I wasn't keen on surgery either, so mum took me to see Dr Williams who was now the family GP, as Dr Walker had retired, and asked him his opinion. He said something along the lines of 'your son is being treated by a very good specialist and I am not qualified to question her opinion, expertise and advice – if it was my son I would probably have it done'. Mum and dad accepted this and decided that I would have the operation.

Before I could be admitted to hospital to undergo surgery it was necessary to check I wasn't carrying any infection and visited Dr Williams to have a throat swab. He inserted a long wooden stick with a sterile cotton wool swab on the end into my mouth and wiped it over my throat. This he placed in a glass tube which he sealed and sent away for testing.

When the results came back they showed that I had an infection. The surgery on my foot was cancelled, but it was decided that my tonsils should come out instead! I was whisked into Frome Victoria Hospital – in the very same bed I'd been in on my first visit! My tonsils were removed and I suffered nothing more than a slight sore throat. I was discharged a few days later and made a speedy recovery. At least I now had experience of surgery, which would bear me in good stead for what was to come later. Not only was it less unpleasant than I'd feared, I also got to eat plenty of ice cream and soft milky puddings.

We often visited mum's parents, my Gran and Gramf Weaver, but I remember one particular visit extremely well. It was the first time, as far as I can recall, I had been to a special celebration. I had no idea what a golden wedding was, but I knew it was important as everyone made a big fuss and dressed up in posh new clothes. Mum took extra special care about how Brian, Margaret and I looked. We wore our best clothes, our shoes were polished to perfection and our hair was combed immaculately. Although I only had one pair of boots that had to be worn everyday and had taken quite a battering, they were polished until they shone. Mum was especially firm with me as she tied my tie and told me to 'stand still and stop wriggling'. Mum and dad looked really nice and smart as well. I had never known a day like it.

The celebration was held in the school in Peasedown St John, almost opposite Gran and Gramf's house in Bath Road. The school was laid out as if for a grand birthday party, with food and cakes on the tables. Everyone sat down, and we had to be quiet and behave and eat what was put in front of us, and not pick and mess about. What a struggle this was! I had never seen so much food. Despite my poor appetite, even I managed to get some down, especially the jelly and cakes.

I was introduced to lots of grown-ups I didn't know – all very tedious and embarrassing – but there were also lots of children there, some of whom I knew. Great, I thought – I can go outside and play in the big playground as soon as I can get away from this table. The grown-ups were just chatting about a lot of stuff I didn't understand, and then one or other of them would get up and say something and everyone would clap. I kept asking mum to let me go outside and play, but was told to be quiet.

At last I was allowed out. It was really good with so many children to join in with. We played football, climbed on things, had a game of hide and seek, and then suddenly everyone disappeared and I was left on my own. Some of them said they were having their photograph taken but I was quite happy to carry on playing on my own and wait for them to return.

Mum then appeared looking rather cross, and saying, 'come at once – we need you for the photograph'.

'I don't want to', I replied.

Mum grabbed me and gave me a shake. 'Just look at you', she said, 'you look like a little ruffian. How did you get into such a mess in such a short time?'

She dragged me screaming and shouting to join everyone outside the school where they were having a group photograph taken. I just didn't want to be in it – it was boring and I wanted to play.

In the rush, mum didn't have time to tidy me up from my dishevelled look, and so a few days later, when our copy of the photographs arrived, I got another telling off. 'Look at you in this picture', my mum scolded, pointing to me standing in the front row, 'you have spoiled it – the occasion has been ruined by you – I

The golden wedding photograph – spot the little ruffian!

am so embarrassed – I will never have one of those photographs in my house'.

I was quite crestfallen, especially when I took a look at the photograph and saw myself as others saw me.

Three years after leaving the orthopaedic hospital, in the late summer of 1948, I had another throat swab, which came back clear, and so I was admitted to B ward at the Bath & Wessex Orthopaedic Hospital. This had around forty beds for boys and girls between eight and ten years old. I soon settled in and made friends with several of the boy patients, who gave me the low down on the house rules. The quicker you understood where you fitted in the better, as there was a pecking order which you needed to know about if you wanted to avoid any unnecessary problems or bullying. My previous experience of hospitals also came in handy here.

The ward sister came to see me on the afternoon I arrived and told me that my foot operation was to be the following day and I needed to be got ready. First, I had to take a bath, so I undressed and removed my callipers, and was wheeled to the bathroom. When the nurse who was supervising me was satisfied I had washed myself thoroughly, she took a safety razor and shaved my left leg from foot to thigh. She told me this was to ensure that no germs or infections were present before surgery. A staff nurse was summoned to inspect my leg and ensure that all the hair had been removed and I was wheeled back to bed. I had nothing to eat for the rest of the day and very little to drink.

Early next morning I was taken into the treatment room, dressed in a white gown, laid on a trolley and given a pre-med injection, which I was told would make me sleepy. The ward sister and nurse were really kind, holding my hand and comforting me. This really helped me to remain calm and overcome my fear and anxieties. Then a porter arrived dressed in a green gown and wheeled me into the operating theatre.

'Philip – wake up – it's all over', was the next thing I remember. A nurse was sitting by me smiling and tapping my face.

'Would you like a drink?' she asked.

I nodded.

'Small sips only', she said, holding the glass to my lips.

I was so thirsty that, before she could stop me, I took a deep gulp of the cool water – and was promptly sick! The rest of the day passed in a kind of haze.

The following day I was woken up, washed and propped up in bed. I was in a small room next to the treatment room. There was a girl who had also had an operation in the bed alongside me.

The pain in my foot was so bad that I was given tablets, but they made no difference. A liquid painkiller was tried but this too brought no relief. No matter what I was given, the pain in my foot was agonising. It was checked every few hours and the blood stains on the dressing marked with an indelible pencil to ensure that the flow of blood had stopped.

When the girl was well enough to be taken back to the ward, I was left in the recovery room on my own. I was in constant pain and now I had no one to talk to. I wanted to get back to the ward and decided to pretend, by singing and appearing as happy as I could, that the pain had gone away. This not only had the desired effect of getting me back to the ward – I am sure that being cheerful despite the pain helped me overcome it.

Although the pain gradually eased, it never completely went away, and I have suffered with pain in my left foot ever since. This is probably due to the extent of the surgery and the unusual amount of tendon and bone grafting involved, which left the foot in a fixed position. However, it is only fair to point out I have had several operations since and this was the only one which caused me any real pain. I would also like to reassure anyone who reads this not to refuse surgery, because in the main it is relatively pain-free.

After about ten days the splint and bandages were removed from my foot and lower leg and the stitches were removed. This was not particularly unpleasant and the nurse sat me up to watch what she was doing. I was then taken to the plaster room to have a walking plaster fitted to my foot and leg up to the knee – my toes were left peeping though the plaster cast. A metal tube was inserted into the heel section of the plaster so that I could still wear my callipers. Then I was sent back to the ward for the plaster cast to harden.

Everyone in the ward had their temperatures taken every day. If anyone had a raised temperature, this meant they had picked up an infection, and a course of injections was prescribed to clear it up. As the injections were into the buttocks everyone wanted to avoid this at all costs. As many of us had considerable experience of hospitals, we knew what was considered an acceptable temperature, and to make things even easier the thermometers had a small arrow on them indicating the optimum temperature. We also knew, because we had seen the nurses do it many times, that if a thermometer was shaken downwards the mercury would fall and give a lower reading. So we kept checking the readings and if they went over the mark we shook them downwards. We also held the thermometers in our mouths and not under our tongues once we had achieved a suitable result. This was quite a good game but it was not always possible to outwit the nurses and sometimes we were watched more carefully than others – it was a case of doing it without getting caught. If you were you were reported to the ward sister and the riot act followed.

On one occasion a lad named Desmond had a temperature and he continually refused his injections. There was no way he could get away without them but the nurse was unable to obtain his co-operation. He just refused and screamed and shouted. There was a staff nurse who was very strict. We nicknamed her 'Jezebel', and it was she who was called in, along with two other nurses, to deal with Desmond. Without bothering to pull the screens around the bed, which was standard practice, she stripped the clothes from his bed and, with the two nurses holding him down, took the syringe from the medicine tray, plunged it into Desmond's exposed buttocks and returned it to the tray before he could shout 'ouch'. I have never seen anything happen so quickly. Needless to say it was a lesson to us all. I don't recall anyone refusing an injection again, including Desmond!

We had many games and challenges in Ward B – one of these was to get a goodnight kiss from a nurse before lights out each night. Some of the nurses would do it without any prompting – others were more difficult and needed encouragement! Many of the nicer ones used to say, 'come into my arms like a bundle of charms', followed by a kiss and a cuddle. The object of the game was to collect a list of nurses who had kissed you. Some proved almost impossible, usually the more strict and unpleasant ones. I did however eventually get a kiss off Jezebel. I am not sure how I persuaded her but I did (must have been my irresistible charm!).

Many boys were jealous of my achievement and I think I went up in the pecking order.

By the time Christmas arrived, I was going to the gym and learning to walk again. I was doing quite well and, although my foot kept hurting, I tried to say as little as possible about it, but just kept on trying. We all helped to decorate the ward. When Christmas Day arrived, we all had presents to open and the ward was alive and buzzing with joy and laughter – for this one special day it didn't seem like a hospital at all. The nurses and sisters seemed in a really good mood and were all very nice to us. Come dinnertime a huge turkey was wheeled into the ward accompanied by Miss Forrester-Brown dressed as a fairy and John Bastow dressed as a sailor! They both carved the turkey and then we tucked into our Christmas dinner.

What really sticks in my mind was Miss Forrester-Brown smiling and joking –the first and only time I ever saw her do this – she was always so intense, but a brilliant specialist.

When I left hospital early in the spring of 1949, I had to stay at home to build my strength up. Anything beyond a little gentle play was out of the question and school was off the agenda for the foreseeable future. About six months after the operation I went to the clinic to have my plaster removed. This was done with a long-handled tool, something like a tree-lopper. The jaws of the instrument were forced under the plaster of Paris casing to cut it

Christmas 1948: John Bastow dressed as a sailor,
Miss Forrester-Brown dressed as a fairy

off – a long drawn out and somewhat uncomfortable procedure. Once the plaster was removed a very skinny leg and foot covered in flaking skin was exposed. My leg was cleaned up and I was taken home and put straight in the large tin bath – the first bath I'd had for six months, as it had been imperative that the plaster cast didn't get wet.

During my bath we discovered that one of the stitches had been left in my leg. When we went to see our GP about it he advised mum to apply Friar's Balsam daily to prevent infection and wait for it to fall out. It didn't, so after about a week, when I'd been in the bath again, mum and I decided to try to remove it. As I'd seen stitches removed, I explained to her how they did it in hospital. I told her she needed tweezers and small scissors, which had to be sterilised in boiling water. I then pulled the stitch tight with the tweezers, mum cut it and I pulled it out as quickly as I could. The whole operation was over in a flash and was virtually painless.

It had been impressed on me that I must never put any weight on my left leg without my callipers on. But I wanted to walk normally. When I was in my bedroom on my own – Brian used to come to bed later as he was two-and-a-half years older – I would practise walking without my irons. My bed was close to the windowsill and I would stretch my arms out to the bed and windowsill and use them for support as I took a few steps. Gradually I lifted my arms up and began to walk unaided. It was magic. No one knew what I was doing. Within a few months I could walk around the bedroom. This was my secret.

This had been going on for some time. I was quite confident and really wanted to tell someone. Then, at my monthly clinic, I finally had a chance to demonstrate my prowess. The specialist asked me to walk without my irons. I whipped them off and I was away. He said nothing except, 'good – put your callipers back on'. My mum asked me on the way home, 'have you walked without your irons before?'

'Yes', I replied, 'lots of times'.

She smiled gently. My secret had been rumbled.

I returned to school – initially just for morning sessions – a few days later.

CHAPTER FIVE

Taking on the Bullies

I was almost nine when I returned to Wesley Junior School. It stood among a small group of buildings which included a Methodist church, built in 1810, an infants' school (which I had attended briefly) and the headmaster's house. This school has a strong Whitmarsh tradition – my dad, his brothers and sisters, my brother and sister, and even my oldest son Kevin have all attended it over the years.

Wesley School

Because I had missed so much school I was assigned to the 'Dunces' Class'. This included boys and girls of various ages, and was run by Mrs Sutton, an elderly, kind and very patient teacher. She spent a lot of time helping me with writing, reading and arithmetic. I soon started to gain in confidence and ability despite only attending in the mornings. I remember on one occasion so wanting to impress Mrs Sutton with my maths that I rushed through an 'adding up' test, just putting down any answers, and took it up to her – I wanted to be the first in the class to finish. Speed was important to me and I completely disregarded the consequences!

'That was quick, Philip', she remarked, and sat me down beside her while she marked it. Surprise, surprise – every one was wrong! She just smiled and said, 'you can do better than this, Philip', and told me to go back to my seat and take my time to do it correctly.

This I did and, although I ended up being the last in the class to finish, I did very well.

Despite being part-time, my schoolwork continued to improve and I soon returned to a normal class with boys and girls of my own age, including several long-standing friends. My handwriting was really poor, however, and Mr Weeks, my new teacher, gave me some help and advice, together with additional practice work. He also supplied me with a nice new 'dip in' pen and fresh ink, which I had to hand back to him after each session for safekeeping.

Then the bullying started. I was called names such as stiff leg, iron leg, hop-along and cripple. My cap was pulled off and kicked and thrown around the playground. I was pushed over, tripped up and punched – my attackers would then run away shouting 'Ha! Ha! Can't catch me!' or 'Come on, slow coach!' Other children would pull faces and give me a hard time. More and more of them started to join in. Every day seemed to be worse. I didn't complain or tell anyone – I just knew it had to stop, and I was determined to stop it. One thing I was certain of – I would not give in. I seemed to have no fear of what would happen to me, just a determination to beat those who were treating me like this. Whoever gave me grief, I attacked, punched, or told them what I thought of them. I asked them why they were doing it. All the boys involved were bigger than me – I was so skinny and bony – but I still took them on.

At the same time I was building strong friendships with several boys living near me. Some of them would stick up for me – others would offer to catch my assailants. Here at least was a glimmer of hope – yet I knew that, however much support I had, in the end I had to look out for myself. My friends would not always be around.

The main problem was that I could not catch the name-callers. Occasionally I managed to grab one of them if he came too close, but they could all run faster than me. With one stiff callipered leg, I could only hop and skip. I could propel myself along at an amazing speed but it still wasn't fast enough. I had to devise a scheme. I decided that leaving school as soon as the bell went and lying in wait for my assailants was the best course of action.

Butts Hill, the road leading from the school to my home in The Butts, had houses with high walls and gateways with large stone pillars which provided a perfect hiding place. So, having left school ahead of the majority of children, I waited here for a bully to come past. I would then ambush him with tremendous gusto, catching him completely by surprise. I would either give him a punch or two, or just ask why he was treating me as he was. Most of the bullies

I confronted in this way had no answer. I was astonished how many of them became quite frightened and cowardly once they were tackled on their own. I would tell them to 'STOP IT!' often following this up

The gateways on Butts Hill – ideal for a small boy to lie in wait for his assailants

with some comment such as 'you never know what you may be like one day – I haven't always been like this!' Gradually, most of the bullies learnt to turn their attention to easier targets. Some even became my friends!

As I moved into the final year of junior school, I was still way behind my classmates, but, although the eleven-plus examinations were looming, it didn't really bother me that only about six or seven from our class of forty would go on to grammar school. I had no particular desire to go there – we called those who went 'Grammar Grubs' as if they were some kind of weirdoes! This, in my case at least, was due to ignorance. I often wish I had known the importance of a grammar-school education, but it was never explained to me and no one made any effort to give me extra tuition to see if I could catch up.

I was now attending school full time. Previously, I had had to rest lying on my stomach for several hours each afternoon. I also had to do repetitive exercises to strengthen my back. Mum made sure I did them without cheating, as she knew I would skip a few given the chance. Miss Forrester-Brown was concerned about my back and had prescribed this regime to prevent curvature of the spine. She was also concerned about my pronounced limp which meant that I was constantly leaning heavily to the left, placing more strain on my back. Even when I returned to school full time, I still had to rest for an hour on my stomach during the early afternoon lesson.

One day – a damp, drizzly, overcast sort of day – I am strolling dreamily towards the cloakroom to collect my raincoat before I set off home for lunch. For the first time I am beginning to enjoy school. I can finish work on the same day instead of it taking several days, and often never getting finished at all. Suddenly there is a new meaning to school; today I have even stayed behind for a few minutes to complete some artwork I'm particularly pleased with. Most of the others have left and the school is very quiet, almost as though I've got the place to myself.

My mind drifts to what I am going to have for lunch. My mum and dad despair over my eating habits – or lack of them. I just don't eat very much – a few mouthfuls and that's it. Is it going to be one of mum's fantastic steamed apple suet puddings flavoured with cloves? I like to see how many cloves I can find in my portion – hoping to collect more than my brother or sister! Will I be able to eat enough dinner to have a pudding, I wonder? To encourage me to eat, mum often says that I'll get no pudding if I leave my dinner. Usually, though, I get pudding anyway as mum is really pleased to see me eat anything heartily. I don't push my luck too far though!

Because of my poor appetite I'm very thin and considered to be rather frail. One of my friends says that 'you could play God Save the King' on my ribs because they're so prominent. I don't mind, though – he's a good friend and playmate. Apart from one other lad I'm the shortest boy in my class. I only discovered I was no longer the shortest when we were last measured and our heights marked on the classroom wall. I was a quarter inch taller than the shortest.

Brian and Margaret and me, just back from Sunday School and looking spick and span, I wasn't only the second shortest boy in my class - I was also shorter than Margaret, two years my junior

Was I proud of that!

I go into the cloakroom and reach for my raincoat.

Suddenly I am dragged to the floor by a lad who sits astride me and starts punching me in the face. I recognise him as one of the bullies I've had regular encounters with. I can't move! I don't feel afraid – just concerned at how I'm going to get out of this. He's obviously enjoying it. The grin on his face is menacing – he thinks I'm totally helpless and in his power.

Many thoughts race through my head – what shall I do, what can I do? I cannot move – my arms are trapped. I have to get out of this! I'm not afraid, just determined to put an end to this. If only I was bigger and stronger! Perhaps I should have eaten my dinners. Blows and punches continue to rain down on me. I must get out of this! Yes I must get out!

He stops punching me, wraps his legs around my chest and crosses his feet behind my back. I'm in the dreaded 'scissors grip'. Breath is being squeezed from my body. The pain is excruciating

– worse than before – or is it? My hands are free! I have a chance! As if I've suddenly gained new strength from somewhere, I manage to wriggle free.

Despite having one leg in callipers I'm up on my feet faster than my attacker. Perhaps he's worn himself out – I don't know and I don't care! Before he has time to scramble to his feet, I grab a handful of his hair with my left hand, pull his head towards me and punch him on the nose as hard as I can. There is a stunned silence! Blood begins to spurt from his nose. The fight is over.

I pick up my raincoat and leave. I don't look back, I don't hurry, I'm simply going home for my dinner. Behind me all remains quiet.

At home I sit and eat my dinner, feeling quite normal. Although I'm later than usual no questions are asked. I'm not angry, I'm not afraid – this is, I tell myself, just a normal day – and no suet pudding, more's the pity.

I get back to school just in time. I don't live far away but I walk quite slowly and always take a long time over my food. I sit down at my desk. Everything seems normal – why shouldn't it?

The door from the headmaster's study opens directly into our classroom. After a few minutes it opens, the headmaster walks out and beckons me over. I get up, walk over, quite unconcerned, and go into the study. Not a word is spoken. I don't even wonder why I need to see him, or, for that matter, why he wants to see me. I have never been into his study before, yet I am quite calm. He's always been kind to me – why should I be concerned?

As I enter the study I am met with a pathetic sight. My bullying attacker is there with his mother, looking decidedly dejected. Serve him right, I think to myself! I soon learn that he's been to hospital. The bleeding didn't respond immediately to treatment and has had to be plugged with cotton wool. His bloodied nose looks huge. It seems to obliterate his face.

The headmaster turns to me.

'Have you been in a fight, Philip?'

'Yes Sir'.

'Why have you done this?' he asks, frowning deeply.

'Because I am always being hit, punched, beaten, pushed around, called names such as peg-leg and iron leg. It's all the time! I'm fed up with it! I hate it! If he does it to me again I will punch him again.'

I'm not scared or frightened, just determined to stop these beatings! For the first time I have the chance to say how I feel.

The headmaster turns to my opponent.

'Is this true?' he asks.

He nods feebly.

The headmaster takes my assailant and barks at him to bend over the desk. He takes his cane and proceeds to cane him in front of his mother and me.

The headmaster tells me to return to the classroom and say nothing to anyone, explaining that it's a matter between the four of us.

'If anyone asks what happened, just refer them to me' is his parting shot as I walk out of the study.

I return to my desk and carry on with my work. Nobody asks me what happened in the headmaster's study. Nobody comments on the bully's absence from class, even when it continues for several days.

To this day I have never told anyone his name. He knows, my headmaster and his mother knew, and of course I know. The story has been told a few times in recent years, but never ever will I name him. Justice had been done – although now, in an odd sort of way, I feel rather sorry for him!

I was ten years old when this happened, and this was when the bullying and name-calling suddenly seemed to stop. I'm not sure why. Perhaps it became common knowledge that, small though I was, I wasn't going to be pushed around. I would never give in. I never would accept it. I just wanted to be treated as a normal boy, to join in and do what all the other kids did.

I now know this was the first major turning point in my life.

It was also the last real physical fight I ever had – admittedly there were a few skirmishes along the way, but nothing after I left school. And, although I was small and relatively weak at the time, I soon started to increase in stature, especially after leaving school.

One problem was that, if I were to shed my callipers – which I was absolutely determined to do – my left leg would be vulnerable in any fights. It was so wasted, weak and devoid of muscle, a serious break could result in amputation or an even more severe disability. And if it wasn't protected by a leg iron it was likely to be broken or severely damaged in any serious encounter. I needed to wise up! Up till now I had been lucky, but I knew that my luck wouldn't last for ever. Some self discipline and a new approach was required.

What I had discovered, when in disagreements with bullies, was that you needed to be quick and firm. I couldn't run away from trouble. If I was 'in it' I was 'in it'. There was no easy escape, no alternative but to face the music. I realised that timing and the first punch were vital. The first punch is the only one you seem to feel. That's my opinion, anyway; perhaps I was lucky.

I had begun to realise that, when an argument peaked, just before a fight started, if I moved towards my opponents they always moved back. I suppose this was an instinctive reaction – I was encroaching on their territory. The move back was the signal. When they launched themselves towards me, their forward motion combined with my fist swinging towards them created, if my timing was right, a magnificent punch. It always seemed to stop them in their tracks anyway.

Perhaps I had been lucky, or assisted by some divine force – I don't know – but I knew that, with my leg the way it was, this was a dangerous path to follow. Something needed to change – and it now dawned on me that I had a weapon that, if used properly, could be just as devastating as my fist – my tongue!

Age ten – how could someone with such an angelic face punch so hard?

Yes, I was developing stronger powers of argument, persuasion and influence to get me out of tight spots. I was beginning to really stand up for myself and learning skills that could make a real difference to my circumstances. This became extremely useful as I grew up and met new challenges. As they say, 'there is more than one way to skin a cat'. I needed to know what outcome I required, and then aim to achieve it in a controlled and intelligent way, and be really determined about the final result. In effect, I started to have ambitions and targets to aim at.

It was about this time that I joined the Life Boys. It was great to join in with boys outside of school, both from Wesley and other Frome schools. They put on a play and I was given the part of an old lady – my limp made it easy for me to appear old and infirm! The perfect part? I had to carry an armful of parcels and my opening line was 'Oh dear! Oh dear! I have so far to go'. On the first night I did not get very far – just a few shaky steps – before the umbrella I was using as a walking stick snapped in two with a resounding crack. I only just managed to stop myself falling flat on my face as the parcels fell all over the stage and the play came to an abrupt halt amid hoots of laughter. Unfortunately, soon after this the Life Boys

Just after joining the Life Boys in 1950 - I am on the far left without a uniform

were disbanded – although this was totally unconnected with my somewhat inauspicious launch into the world of amateur dramatics.

The day of the eleven-plus arrived. Some parts I found quite easy, other parts were very hard. Only seven of us passed, and I wasn't one of them. In hindsight I suppose that was inevitable because of the amount of schooling I'd missed. And so, when we broke up for the summer holidays, I knew, along with most of my friends, I'd be going to Oakfield Secondary Modern.

CHAPTER SIX

Catching Up

Oakfield Secondary Modern was fairly new, having opened in 1940, the year I was born. Among its 400 or so pupils was Brian, who was three years ahead of me. It was more than a mile from my home, and, as this was considered too far for me to walk, I had to catch the school bus.

On the first day, I was taken round the school, along with the other new pupils, by Mr Ward. A former army PT instructor, he was not only the assistant headmaster, but also senior PE teacher and senior maths teacher. He was well known as a strict but fair teacher, often outspoken and with a strong sense of humour. He had a gift for bringing out the best in his pupils, but wasn't prepared to put up with any nonsense. As a result, most pupils either liked him or hated him – there were no half measures where he was concerned.

As he showed us round the school he explained the rules – no running in the corridors, no walking on the grass, no shouting, and we had to act like adults, not children, now that we were in the big school. At the end of the tour we were all amazed at how big the school was, compared to the ones we had come from. Some of us wondered if we would ever manage to find our way around. Mr Ward, however, gave us a useful tip, explaining how the room numbers ran; if we remembered where the highest and lowest numbered rooms were, it would be a simple process to find any classroom we required.

As if we weren't awestruck enough by this point, his final words to us left us in no doubt where we stood. 'You are no longer the biggest pupils in the school', he began, 'you are the smallest.

Oakfield School

Many of the pupils here are young adults, just remember that. You are no bigger than half a worms eye' – and to emphasise the point he held up his hand with thumb and forefinger almost but not quite meeting and glared at each of us in turn. No one escaped his stony gaze – it was as though he was looking right into your soul. We all, without exception, received his message loud and clear. For some, this was the start of a loathing that was to last throughout their schooldays and beyond, but even then I felt there was, under all the strictness, an unmistakable warmth to this extraordinary character.

He then dismissed us and we went to our respective form rooms. I had been placed in 1B1, which was somewhat of a disappointment because most of my friends were in 1A, the highest group. It also brought home to me how far behind many of the others I still was. The B stream was split into two sections – B1 and B2 – and there was also a C stream. Many of the boys and girls in my class were unknown to me, but Phil, the lad I sat with, was from Wesley School and already a friend of mine.

I had been in my new school for less than two months when it was decided that I needed another operation. Miss Forrester-Brown had become increasingly concerned about the uneven growth of my legs. My right leg was now three inches longer than my left, and I had to wear a raised boot which was heavy and cumbersome. If something had not been done the difference would have increased to six inches or more by the time I'd finished growing, and my left leg would have been even weaker.

The growth of my legs had been closely monitored on my monthly visits to the orthopaedic clinic. I needed surgery to slow the growth of my right leg by pinning the growing point of the femur or thighbone. This would give my left leg a chance to catch up. To be effective, though, the operation had to be carried out at a precise time in my growing cycle. That time came in November 1951.

The operation was to be performed by Mr Hedley Hall, who had taken over much of the workload from Miss Forrester-Brown. She was now moving towards retirement and taking on more of a consultancy role. We were introduced to him at the monthly clinic and he impressed both mum and me with his friendly, assured manner – a complete contrast to the rather intense character of his predecessor!

Arrangements were made for the usual throat swab (which was clear) and I was admitted to A Ward at Bath & Wessex Orthopaedic Hospital. This was a boys-only orthopaedic ward with about 40 beds and ages ranging from 11 to 15. All the boys had problems caused by birth defects, polio, TB, injuries and so on, affecting their legs, arms, backs, hands and feet. Some could walk, others could not.

I was shown to my bed where I unpacked my clothes and washing kit and stored them in my locker. Mum wished me well and left for home. I was quite happy in myself and soon made friends with a few of the lads. They soon accepted me once they discovered it was the third time I had been in this hospital, and had been a patient in all of the children's wards. I was also spared the horror stories about life on the ward, as they realised I would probably be unshaken by them, and would have plenty of my own to tell.

One vital factor in orthopaedic care at the time was an abundance of fresh air. Our ward had sliding doors the length of one side, overlooking open lawns, and these were rarely closed. If the sun shone all the beds were wheeled onto the concrete verandah, but irrespective of the weather the doors were open virtually all the time. I had snow on my bed on more than one occasion, and following a heavy frost I was used to finding the lemonade or Tizer on my bedside table frozen, with the bottle shattered. To ensure we didn't get too cold, we were all issued with mittens, balaclavas and other items of warm clothing before lights out, and most of us buried ourselves under the bedclothes for extra warmth. Never do I remember the doors being closed because of the cold – the only time they were pulled to was if there was heavy rain blowing onto our beds.

The first night in the ward was an amazing experience. As soon as the lights went out everyone who could walk collected books from the book cupboard and handed them out round the ward. One or two lads with arm or hand problems were excused, but as a 'walker' I was called upon to assist. I kept asking what was happening but was just told to keep quiet and get on with handing the books out.

Once they'd all been distributed, Jimmy, who at around 15 was one of the oldest boys on the ward, shouted 'go'. This was the signal for books to start flying across the ward in all directions. Most went wide of the mark, but occasionally someone would get hit. It was pandemonium! Someone kept watch to make sure no nurses were coming and at any sign of danger a quick 'stop' would be hissed out. This worked like a charm, and even though the occasional nurse popped her head round the door, thinking she had heard something, everything seemed perfectly innocent and quiet, and she soon went away. I am not sure what the object of the game was – whether it was to hit someone or just to see how long we could go on before getting caught – and nobody ever bothered to enlighten me. Fortunately, more by luck than judgement, no one was seriously injured.

The book fight lasted for an hour or so before fizzling out, after which most of us dropped off to sleep – only to be awoken by lights blazing and voices raised as a bevy of nurses stormed into the ward, headed by the night sister waving her arms and shouting, 'what's this? – get this ward cleared up!' Everyone who was able to walk was ordered out of bed to pick up and put away the books. The ward was soon tidy and we all went back to sleep. Somewhat surprisingly, there was never any enquiry into what had happened and little was said. I never experienced another book fight, though.

The next morning I was given a bath and my right leg was carefully shaved and inspected by the ward sister. As my operation was to be the following day, I had nothing to eat after a light lunch and no drinks after lights out.

The next morning I was taken into the treatment room and dressed in a white gown. Large white woolly bed socks were pulled onto my legs and a white hat placed on my head. I was then given a pre-med injection and, with a smile of encouragement from the nurse, left to rest. Then, when the porter arrived, I was lifted onto a trolley, covered in blankets and wheeled off to the operating theatre.

'Come along Philip', is the next thing I hear. A nurse is holding my hand and smiling at me. 'Your operation is over', she tells me. I look around. I am back in the recovery room and, apart from the nurse, all alone.

'What time is it?' I ask.

Why I wanted to know the time is beyond me, but for some reason every time I've had surgery since, this is the first almost instinctive question I've always asked after I've come round. Perhaps it's because I'm aware that surgery always entails a certain risk and that I've returned from a close encounter with the unknown – or even a brush with death. So asking the time is no more than an expression of relief.

After I was fully awake, I realised that I was in no pain whatsoever – in total contrast to the operation on my foot! What a tremendous relief that was! I was soon feeling much better and returned to the ward the following day. This was also a relief, as it was obviously much more fun to be back with the boys than on my own in the recovery room.

Now that the operation was over and my anxieties behind me, it was time to settle into the daily routine of the ward – and also to try to introduce a bit of variety. I'd noticed that there was no 'goodnight kiss' challenge, so, drawing on my extensive hospital experience, I decided to introduce it. I knew nurses were likely to be particularly kind to you after operations, and this gave me an advantage. Just before lights out, a nurse came to make sure I was comfortable and see if I needed anything. I told her everything was fine, but that, to ensure I had a good night's rest, a goodnight kiss might help. Naturally, she complied, and so the contest was inaugurated. It lasted for the whole of my time in Ward A, and I clocked up an almost 100% success rate, although I never managed to get one off the ward sister. To their dismay, many of the older boys failed to achieve anything like this tally. Perhaps they tried too hard, perhaps it was down to my charm – or their lack of it – who knows?

After about ten days my stitches were removed and I was fitted with a full-length walking plaster. I now had a real problem to overcome – walking with two stiff legs! I had daily sessions in the gym to regain my balance and learn to walk again by using parallel bars. After a few days I was able to get around with the aid of a walking frame. A week or so later, I was eventually able to walk with no assistance. The only problem was that I was much slower than before – but I could live with that! Mobility was the prize!

On one of my mum's visits, she told me that her mother, Granny Weaver, had died. This really upset me. She was so kind and used to cuddle me and say, 'you sit with your gran'. It was the first time I ever remember someone I loved dying. Mum put her arm around me and held me whilst I shed a few tears. What made me even more upset was that it seemed a very, very long time since I had seen her and I sadly realised I would never see her again.

During the time I was confined to bed I took part in the bed races that the less mobile boys resorted to. If you swung back and forward from the waist vigorously enough, and got the timing right, it was remarkable how far and fast you could propel your bed across the ward. The only problem was that it was impossible to make them go in a straight line, so the races ended up with beds all over the place, which obviously incurred the wrath of the nurses and sisters. We even managed to get our beds outside onto the verandah, the problem with this being the impossibility of getting them back inside again. Sometimes we were left out there as a punishment – not much fun if it started raining – although we could generally persuade some of the 'walkers' to push us back.

My education while in hospital wasn't entirely neglected, although it was of a very rudimentary nature. With only one teacher for around 40 boys of widely different abilities and ages, it could hardly have been otherwise. Most of us had to work alone with just the odd bit of supervision. There was little discipline, and we often used to play around. Another problem was that many of us had to leave the ward during lessons to go to the gym, receive treatment or have our dressings changed. In the run up to Christmas 1951, most of our lessons were occupied with making paper chains, painting twigs, pinecones and so on to decorate the ward. By the time Christmas Eve arrived the ward looked fantastic – but it did little to help my schooling.

On Christmas Day, as well as presents from friends and family, every boy in the ward received a mouth organ, unless he already had one. We had a ward cleaner and handyman who played this instrument brilliantly. He was always prepared to entertain us, and it was such a joy to hear him we all wanted to play as well. He'd already taught some of the boys to play, and the gift of the mouth organs meant that we all now had a chance. Unfortunately I never managed to get anything that sounded like a tune out of mine and I was convinced there was something wrong with it. When our mentor tried it out, however, he made it sound superb. I persevered for a while, but, after failing to make any progress, eventually resigned myself to failure!

As my walking improved, I helped the nurses to serve meals and drinks. I also helped with bedpans and bottles, especially if one of the boys needed one urgently. This meant I had access to the 'sluice', the room where bottles and bedpans were stored and emptied. The nurses often used to have private chats down there, away from the supervision of the ward sister. One day, I was down there with a couple of other boys when we came across a love letter to a nurse. Perhaps she'd been disturbed while reading it and left it behind in her haste. Anyway, we found it hilarious and were soon reading bits out to each other, when suddenly I felt a firm hand on my shoulder, and, with a curt 'I'll take that', it was snatched away by an irate staff nurse.

We were ordered back to bed with instructions not to move, and shortly afterwards were summoned to the ward sister's office. She reprimanded us fiercely, laying down the law about how wrong it was to read or take other people's letters. Our punishment was banishment to the girls' ward for the next three nights. We were sent back to our beds, where we had to remain for the rest of the day, with the nurses and sisters treating us like pariahs. This was very uncomfortable, especially as the other boys thought it superb fun and took the mickey out of us mercilessly. ,

Just before lights out all three of us were wheeled off to the girls' ward and our beds parked in the middle of the ward. As soon as the lights were out the girls wanted to know what we had done to be punished in this way. We explained about the love letter and quoted bits of it – 'the way you look into my eyes … your lovely smell … your soft lips … the way you cuddle me … I'm the luckiest man on earth … I miss you so much' – which caused so much merriment that the night nurses came in on more than one occasion to tell us to go to sleep.

By the time morning arrived we had built up a healthy friendship with the girls and were really quite enjoying ourselves – it had certainly been a much more pleasant experience than we had feared. The more the girls had asked us the more we'd told them – even going so far as to embellish the odd detail here and there. We were greatly looking forward to the next two nights and started drawing up plans to add even more spicy details to our story. The nurses, however, had different ideas. We had totally disrupted the girls' ward, and they told us so in no uncertain terms. We never found out what report went back to the ward sister, but there was little doubt that we had turned a punishment into a pleasure and had come out on top. Needless to say, we didn't return to the girls' ward that night or the night after. Even better, no alternative punishment was arranged. We were all chuffed at this, especially as our exploits had given us extra kudos among the boys on the ward.

By now it was early spring and my stay in hospital was drawing to a close. It would be another month before my plaster could come off but I was walking so well that I was told I'd be going home early. Then came the business with the glider. It was an unseasonably warm and sunny day and most of us 'walkers' were outside playing on the lawn and verandah. We had a variety of planes and gliders, some homemade, and some superior ones bought from the shops. We were having a great time – some of them flew really well. As our expertise increased we sent them further and further – which meant, of course, that we had to go further and further to retrieve them. Everything was going fine until one of us sent a glider flying over a six-foot wall at the end of the verandah by the men's ward.

We talked over what we should do. It would be a pity to lose one of our finest gliders, yet nobody came forward to scramble over the wall and get it back. So, after checking that nobody was keeping an eye on us, I decided that I would go. The wall was covered in ivy, which meant there was plenty to hold onto to pull me up, and as a result of having to pull myself around for years my arms were very strong.

I was given a bunk up, and despite having two stiff legs – one in plaster and one in callipers – I managed to climb up and over the wall and return the glider. Fortunately, the land on the other side was higher, so it was easy to climb back up, but once over I found myself in a serious dilemma, hanging from the top of the wall, unable to climb down, and still a long way from the ground! Various suggestions were made, but little in the way of assistance. I was in a real fix and eventually had to let myself go. I asked someone to catch me, but to no avail. I landed heavily and there was a loud crack as my plaster gave way just below the knee. A few of the boys scarpered with comments such as 'you're in trouble' as one of my friends helped me back to bed. It wasn't long before someone squealed on me and the ward sister came along to inspect the damage.

Arrangements were made for me to have my plaster repaired and the ward sister called me into her office to give me a good talking to. I was confined to bed for several days as a punishment and told that I wouldn't be going home until the plaster came off. When mum visited me the following weekend, the sister had a word with her before she came into the ward, and she gave me another serious talking to. She was as upset as I was that I wouldn't be going home for another month. 'Look what you've done', was her parting shot, 'I hope you're proud of yourself'. That really hit home. My face was red and I knew that I had really overstepped the mark this time.

Eventually it was time for the plaster to come off, to reveal my right leg covered in flaky skin, with two nicely-healed scars, each about six inches long, on either side of my knee. Although I could walk quite easily, my leg was very stiff and it was very difficult for me to bend my knee. I was taken to the gym and, after the physiotherapist had told me to lie on my stomach, she started bending my knee vigorously as I squirmed in agony. I went to the gym every day for the next week or so, and every day I argued with the physiotherapist as she ordered me on to my stomach and started bending my knee forcibly against my will. Eventually, I refused to lie down and a compromise was reached, with me sitting on the edge of the couch so that I could watch her bending my knee and she could no longer catch me unawares. We made good progress and after a few days of this, it became much easier and a lot less painful. By the time I was ready to go home I could almost bend my leg normally.

When mum arrived with my clothes to take me home I had a real thrill when she produced a pair of lovely grey trousers that she'd made herself. They fitted really well and I felt very proud and grown up. Better still, my bad leg was covered up and out of sight. Mum had had to make the trousers herself as she could find none to fit me, I was so small. Those were the days, of course, when most boys of my age were still in short trousers. I was lucky she was so good at sewing, knitting and needlework.

CHAPTER SEVEN

Fighting Back

When I returned to school after the Easter holidays in 1952 I had been away for about six months. It took me a few days to settle in but my friends were happy to see me back. They were eager to know what had happened in hospital. Some asked to see the scars – and then wished they hadn't – although some were genuinely interested. I explained that, when I finished growing, hopefully my legs would both be the same length. As the left one was still three inches shorter than the right, this met with some scepticism; I just told them to wait and see. Meanwhile, I set to to make up for lost time, throwing myself into my schoolwork and playing along with the best of them.

Brian, along with some of his friends, was in the St John's Ambulance Brigade, and I sometimes helped him practice using bandages and slings. Having spent so long in hospital, I had first-hand experience of splints, bandages and supports and understood quite a bit about first aid. I joined St John's as soon as I was eleven and for the first time found I had an advantage over my peers. Mr Coombs and Mr Collier, who ran the brigade, seemed to recognise leadership qualities in me and appointed me captain of the junior competition team. They were keen to encourage me and this really spurred me on. It was the first time I had outshone my peers – the first time, perhaps that I had had an even break. I studied all the books and manuals and kept asking questions – I had a thirst to learn and found I could remember all the funny names of bones, complaints and treatments quite easily. It also helped that I was well mannered and polite, something that couldn't be said for some of the other boys. In the first inter-club competition I led my team to

My first ever trophy, as captain of a St John's Ambulance Team, with Ted Brewster on the left and Colin Perry on the right

victory and was so proud to be photographed with my first ever trophy.

Despite my best efforts, however, I was still struggling with my schoolwork. I was so far behind and there was much I didn't understand. My friend Phil helped me try to fill in some of the gaps but for the most part I was simply left to flounder. When end-of-term examinations came along, I had to miss two exams because of orthopaedic appointments. No arrangements were made for me to sit the exams at other times so I scored zero in both subjects. When the results came out I was second from bottom in a class of forty. My parents received a letter informing them that I would probably be moved down to 2C after the summer holidays.

There was, however, one other light on the horizon at this time, which boosted my confidence that I could overcome the barriers thrown in my way – I learnt to swim. I first visited the swimming baths in a double PE lesson. Mr Ward, along with several other sports teachers, marched us down there and, once we had changed into our costumes, he told us to gather at the shallow end.

'Hands up who can swim'.

A dozen hands shot up.

'Right', he shouted, 'you can all swim up to the deep end and someone will keep an eye on you'.

We watched the swimmers dive in and start making their way towards the deep end before he told us to move forward to the edge of the pool.

'At the count of three', he announced, 'I want you to jump in'.

There were a few worried glances, but he assured us that the water wasn't deep and if we got into trouble all we had to do was stand up. To prove his point, he pointed out someone of our own age walking around at the shallow end. Then it was 'one, two, three – jump!' and around 20 kids – me included – hit the water with a resounding splash.

When Mr Ward realised I was among those who'd followed his instructions, he ran over to where I was coming up for air.

'Whitmarsh – are you all right?' he asked anxiously.

'Yes, sir', I replied, although the big grin on my face at having discovered this new freedom rendered any comment superfluous.

'Good – well done – don't frighten me like that again – you could have had some help!'

'I'm all right sir!'

Having recovered his momentary loss of composure, Mr Ward congratulated all of us who had jumped in.

'You have shown you are not afraid of the water', he announced, 'I will have you all swimming within a few weeks'.

A few had been too nervous to take the plunge. These he handed over to another teacher to coax into the water, before spending the rest of the lesson teaching us the basics, such as how to keep our eyes open under water, building up our confidence and removing any lingering fear of the water.

Mr Lee, the superintendent in charge of the swimming baths, was a tubby friendly man who lived almost opposite my home.

Following my first visit to the swimming pool, he took me under his wing, giving me free lessons and encouraging me to go the swimming club, where I would receive expert help and guidance. As a result, it only took about a week before I could swim. This had two fantastic benefits. First, as I soon outstripped most of my schoolmates, I came up with the motto, 'slow on land – fast in water'. I was finally ahead of the pack at something; the 'slowcoach' tag I'd been stuck with for so long suddenly didn't apply any more. Second, swimming made me very hungry. After a few lengths I had this amazing appetite. My eating problems suddenly became a thing of the past and I could eat just about anything. This was a great relief to my mum, who started telling me I was eating more than my father!

My health, strength and well-being increased by leaps and bounds. I don't think I ever looked back or faltered after this. My visits to the physiotherapist were becoming less and less frequent, due to my improved mobility, and it was felt at last that I was really on the road to recovery and normality.

My increased mobility didn't seem to meet with my grandfather's approval, however. One day while visiting him with my mum and Brian and Margaret, I was looking into his shed-cum-workshop and he told me to go away. Some things never changed. I wandered off down the garden keeping a look out to see if he was watching and, when the coast was clear, disappeared behind the runner beans. Just below the protective netting I spied a ripe strawberry, just asking to be picked, so I grabbed it and popped it into my greedy lips with relish – thinking I had managed to outwit him.

I wandered around the garden for a while, trying to look innocent and admiring how neat and productive everything was, before strolling back up towards the house whistling cheerfully. There stood grandfather, as formidable as ever, and as I drew near, ''ad a slug in 'im did 'er?' he asked. My face went red as I flushed full of guilt. Had I been rumbled – or was he just guessing? To this day I'm not sure – although I'm sure the strawberry didn't have a slug in it. Still, it bore out the truth of that old adage, be sure your sins will find you out.

When I returned to school that September I found to my relief that I'd been left in the B stream. Whether the headmaster had considered I'd been unfairly treated or whether – as seems more likely – my parents had intervened, I never discovered, but at least I'd avoided demotion to the lowest grade. This was to be my first full year of uninterrupted schooling and, as I settled in, the difficulties I'd had keeping up seemed to disappear. There were no exams this year, just assessments, but by the end of the year I'd moved from near the bottom of the class to somewhere safely in the middle.

During my second year at Oakfield, however, I experienced a new type of bullying from a teacher, which frankly I found more worrying and unsettling than my other schoolwork difficulties. Our new PE teacher was the problem. He expected me to undertake some activities while excluding me from others. If we practised cricket strokes or the correct way to kick a football, I had to join in, but when we played cricket or football I was left out. I was also left out of sessions in the gym. Worse still, he'd order me to 'go and clear up the changing rooms!' This was a horrible job which involved pairing up and stacking the daps in their correct racks – a thankless and never-ending task. Not only were there hundreds of pairs; after each lesson they were thrown in a heap and had to be sorted all over again. The job was usually given as a punishment, but I'd done nothing wrong. In my eyes I was being victimised which I knew was grossly unfair.

Another example of how this man treated me: my arms were exceptionally strong because I'd had to use them to help me get around. This meant that I was able to throw a cricket ball a considerable distance. There was, in fact, only one boy in my year who ever managed to beat me. When a competition was arranged, however, this PE teacher wouldn't allow me to enter. It came as little surprise when the boy who'd managed to outthrow me won, but he was so far ahead of all the other competitors I'm sure I would have come second at least. Instead, I had to stand by and watch.

I didn't discuss this victimisation with anyone, not even my parents, but, although I never actually devised a scheme to put an end to it, I knew it had to stop. One day I'm in the playing field with my friend Phil during a period of unsupervised exercise, and I announce that I'm going as far away from the changing rooms as possible.

'Why', he asks.

'If I get back to the changing rooms too quick I will have to clear them up. I'm fed up with doing it. I never want to do it again!'

And so, by the time the whistle sounds, we are both at the bottom of the field. We walk back as slowly as possible to make sure we're the last to arrive. The PE teacher is waiting impatiently and, as soon as we get within earshot, 'come on Whitmarsh! hurry up!' he shouts.

I'm the last to roll up. He's furious and pushes me through the door, giving me a kick in the backside for good measure. With no one left outside, he obviously thinks no one will know.

'Clear the changing room up!' he barks.

I wait till I'm right in the changing room, in front of about 40 lads. I turn to face him and reply simply, 'no'.

There is a slight pause before he repeats his command.

'No', I reply again, more defiantly this time.

He gives me a hundred lines – 'I will obey my superiors when I am spoken to' – as punishment.

I refuse to do them.

So it goes on for a little while, with my school mates standing in silence and the number of lines spiralling ever higher. He grows angrier and angrier, but I stand my ground. I eventually end up with five million lines – still I refuse to do them, adding that I don't intend to clear up the changing room ever again. I'm not enjoying this exhibition one bit, but I've got no choice. I'm in it,

I've done nothing wrong and there's no way I'm backing off. I'm also confident that I'm in the right and have no fear of the ultimate outcome.

'Right then, we are off to see the headmaster!' he bawls, in a last desperate attempt to make me cave in.

I open the door into the corridor leading to the headmaster's office.

'And when we get there', I inform him, 'I will tell him you kicked me in the backside!'

No one is more taken aback by this remark than this blustering red-faced fool of a teacher. I have played my trump card and his guilty secret is out in the open. We never do get to go and see the headmaster, nor do I ever have to clear up the changing rooms again. The bell rings to signal the end of the period and he dismisses us before storming off. On the way to our next lesson, my friends laugh and joke about my 'encounter with the enemy'. Another battle over. No longer, I tell myself, will I have to stand on the sidelines or be banished to the changing rooms.

It was soon after this that I became involved in school sports in an unexpected way. The senior cricket team was playing a visiting team and the whole school had turned out to watch. I was walking along the side of the playing field with a few friends when I heard a loud voice say, 'can you score, Whitmarsh?'

It was Mr. Ward.

'What do you mean, sir?' I replied.

He called me over to where he was sitting and explained that, although I might find it difficult to get into the school team, there was no reason why I shouldn't train as the cricket scorer. He took me over to a table where the two cricket scorers, one from each school, were sitting, and sat me down beside them. He told me to watch and learn and went back to watch the match.

There followed a brief introduction to the technicalities of scoring and the importance of acknowledging every signal from the umpire. The two scorers were most helpful and supportive and

I took to the challenge with gusto. At the end of the innings I was given an old scoring book and when the match started again I sat between the two scorers and kept my own record of proceedings. I had to do everything a scorer did, including acknowledging the umpire, and at the end of the match, after my work was checked, I was appointed assistant scorer.

I attended all the matches for the rest of the season to help out and learn the job, in readiness to take over as scorer the following year. This was a fantastic opportunity. Not only did I get to see a lot of cricket and learn a great deal about the game, I was really involved in what was going on and this boosted my confidence enormously. After having suffered the indignity of being excluded on the whim of a bully, I had finally been given the opportunity to take part and – so Mr Ward assured me – make a valuable contribution to the life of the school.

CHAPTER EIGHT

'You've Got a Brain, Whitmarsh'

In September 1953, when I returned to school after the summer holidays, I moved up, along with most of my friends, to 3B. We had a complete change of teachers, which meant that I was rid of my rotten PE teacher. I was especially pleased that Mr Ward would be taking us for both PE and maths. Some of the other teachers also enjoyed good reputations and although none of them had ever taught me I approached the new school year with confidence. I already had a full year's education behind me and no longer had to struggle to keep up with class work.

I continued to get on well with Mr Ward. In PE lessons, he not only involved me in everything that went on but encouraged me to try new challenges. In short, he treated me like a normal boy, which is all I'd wanted all along. Maths classes with Mr Ward also went well and, when it was time to sit a maths exam just before the Christmas break, I felt that I'd given a pretty fair account of myself.

My new-found confidence took a nosedive a few days later when one of the senior boys came to tell me that Mr Ward wanted to see me about my maths paper.

'Oh no, what have I done?' I thought, fearing the worst, and headed for his office.

'Ah, yes! Whitmarsh', was his opening remark, 'your maths paper – you fool!' This knocked me for six. I knew by the tone of his voice he wasn't angry. He seemed, in fact, to find this comment somewhat amusing – although I failed to see the funny side. I thought I was in some sort of trouble but couldn't work out why.

'I don't know what you mean, sir', I replied, suspecting some kind of wind-up.

'You really tested me', he continued, 'I've never seen a maths paper like it. I've never given anyone 100% – fortunately you made one mistake – you've saved my bacon. I've given you 93%. Well done!' He showed me where I'd gone wrong, failing to put a zero after a decimal point in a long division calculation.

'I've marked you quite hard for your one mistake', he admitted, before going on to tell me how well I'd settled down, how I must continue to work hard, and how he admired my incredible determination. Then, adopting a more serious tone, he said, 'you've got a brain, Whitmarsh, I suggest you use it – you won't earn a living digging holes in the road'.

This simple remark had a more profound effect than anything said to me before or since. It was at this moment that I realised that I was better than I thought I was. I wasn't a dunce. I was as good as anyone else. I wouldn't have to do a labouring job. With a few simple words, Mr Ward had turned my life around and opened up a whole new world of possibilities. Children like me from working-class backgrounds didn't tend to go in to white-collar or professional jobs, and I had never considered myself anything more than run of the mill. Now all that had changed. A man I admired and respected was telling me, in effect, that the sky was the limit. Without his influence, I am not sure I would have made it and I am eternally grateful for those few words spoken one winter's

'You've got a brain, Whitmarsh' – Mr Ward from an old school photo

afternoon in a secondary-school office over half a century ago.

The rest of the exams also went really well and when the results were declared I discovered to my astonishment that I'd finished in overall first place. If I'd been told a year earlier, when I'd avoided demotion to the C stream by the skin of my teeth, that by the following Christmas I'd be top of the class, I'd have laughed – along, I suspect, with a good many others – but here I was, going home for the holidays with a letter informing my parents that due to my excellent progress I would be moving up to the A stream when I returned. It was the best Christmas present I could have wished for.

The A stream included many of my close friends, who had been in it since starting at Oakfield, so I quickly settled in. Compared with what I'd been used to, though, some of the lessons were much more difficult and I found myself struggling to keep up. Maths was fine but English was a real challenge. My friends were brilliant in helping me to understand and catch up by lending me their exercise books and explaining and assisting me with any problems I had. I was determined to succeed and wasn't afraid to ask for help.

By now, the operation to reduce the difference in the length of my legs was having the desired effect, and the raised boot I had to wear was much smaller. I was under a new orthopaedic specialist, Tom Price, a really nice man who also wore a raised boot because a birth defect had left him with one leg very much shorter than the other. He understood only too well the handicap caused by wearing specialist footwear and the inconvenience it caused. At one of his monthly clinics he explained that he wanted me to start leaving off my full-length calliper and replacing it with a knee-length one.

A few weeks after being measured for my new calliper, it arrived and I was instructed to wear it initially only for short periods. Once I was confident with it, however, I could discard my long calliper and go on wearing it all the time. The next step would be to start walking without any support at all. The promise of freedom from the constraints of a calliper spurred me on, and within a few days I'd stopped wearing the long calliper for good.

I remember vividly the first time I went to school wearing my short calliper. It was a thrilling moment! I walked into a maths lesson – taken, of course, by my mentor, Mr Ward.

'Philip', he called as I walked towards my desk, 'come here and sit on the edge of my desk'.

I did as I was told and he called the class to order.

'What do you notice different about Philip?' he asked them.

They all looked somewhat puzzled. He'd called me by my Christian name – something he rarely did unless you'd done something outstanding – but even this didn't help them guess what he was driving at. After a few minutes he told everyone to come forward and take a closer look at me. When everyone had gathered round, jostling for position, 'look at his legs', he told them.

At this point the penny dropped and everyone could see that my leg was no longer stiff and stuck straight out in front of me, it was bent normally. The class cheered and clapped and some patted me enthusiastically on the back. What a wonderful moment! I was overwhelmed at my triumph in having cast off my leg irons. It was a very, very special day, and again I have Mr Ward to thank for making it truly memorable.

It wasn't long before I could walk quite easily with or without my short calliper and I believe I only used it for a week or so. I just threw it away onto the local rubbish tip never to wear a leg support again!

Now that I could walk without irons and bend my leg normally I could ride a bike properly for the first time. I had learnt to balance on a bike years earlier but couldn't use the pedals – now I could. I bought a second-hand bike which gave me so much freedom it was fantastic. Before, it had been a hardship just to walk anywhere – now I could go for miles with hardly any effort. As for my train-spotting – a passion just then – I could get to all the best locations, which until now had been too far away. I was so keen on cycling

Just after throwing away my callipers – the hated big boot shows up clearly to compensate for the three-inch difference in the length of my legs

that I decided to try to get a job as a paperboy as soon as I was fourteen.

The bicycle brought another bit of excitement into my life. My grandfather – yes, the one I didn't get on with – gave me a carbide-powered cycle lamp. This was a grand, ancient-looking contraption which inspired envy and curiosity in my schoolmates. Carbide is a substance that looks like small pieces of stone or gravel and gives off an inflammable gas when sprayed with water. It was cheaper than buying batteries and more reliable – better still, nobody else

Clink Road Junction, where trains for Frome branched off the West of England main line and one of the best trainspotting locations in the area

had one. I discovered that if I placed a small piece of carbide in liquid it produced masses of bubbles and froth. Mischievous as ever, I came up with the idea, when no one was looking, of putting a small piece in the inkwells as I was leaving a classroom, especially at lunchtime or after the last lesson in the afternoon. This would give it maximum time to froth. I kept this to myself and it certainly caused a few puzzled looks and questions. I felt a bit like Just William – a particular hero of mine. The cause of the frothing inkwells was never discovered – now I've told the story, I suppose the game is up!

As summer term drew to an end, it was time to prepare for examinations once again. By now I'd been relieved of cricket scoring duties as Mr Ward said it was important for me to concentrate all my efforts on my class work. He also felt I could not afford to miss any more lessons. I'd missed more than enough school in the past and it was important that I grasped every opportunity to improve my education. My results were unbelievable – I finished in overall fifth position out of a class of 37 after only two terms in the A stream.

Shortly afterwards my parents were invited to a parents' evening, where my teachers recommended that I be allowed to stay on past the normal leaving age of 15 to study for GCE O levels. Although my parents were not well off, they agreed. Brian had already left school at 15 to fulfil an ambition he had held since the age of seven of becoming an engine driver on the railway, but my parents realised that, even with the extra money he was bringing in, they wouldn't be able to afford to keep my sister on at school when she reached 15 as well. It was a difficult situation, but, as soon as they reached their decision, my parents sat down with my brother and sister and explained why I was the only one who would be staying on at school.

I'd put my name down with a local newsagent to become a paperboy almost as soon as I got my bike and as I approached my fourteenth birthday – the minimum permitted age – I was given the odd spot of relief work to cover holidays and illness. Finally, I was given a full-time round earning about ten shillings (50 pence) a week, which would help my parents out while I continued at school. It also meant I could buy some of my own clothes and, as I was paying, choose what I wanted. Another freedom – I liked it.

About this time, I started to go fishing more often. My mum was concerned for my safety and often sent Brian to keep an eye on me. I often wondered why he suddenly turned up from nowhere when I was fishing. One day he arrived at a favourite fishing spot of mine which was surrounded by false ground and swamp. I spotted him coming towards me and shouted at him to stop – too late – the next minute he was up to his waist in muddy water. Mum never sent him to spy on me again. I think she realised from this incident that I was quite capable of looking after myself.

I spent a lot of time down at the river, playing as well as fishing, with some of my friends. One day we were on a high bank. One by one my friends took a run-up and jumped across to the other side, where the ground was much lower. Eventually I was the only one left. 'Come on, Phil', they shouted, 'you can do it'. I took a hop and a skip (this was how I tended to run) and leapt energetically towards the far bank when, horror of horrors, my foot caught in some bush and I flopped into the river. The water wasn't deep and I soon managed to clamber out and crawl back up onto the high bank. No way was I going to be defeated, even though my friends were doubled up with laughter at my dilemma. Once at the top, I launched myself across the divide with even more gusto and determination than before and reached the opposite bank without mishap, to claps and cheers from my mates. I was chuffed – even if a bit wet. I had done it! I'd dried out nicely by the time I got home so mum never found out about this particular escapade.

We didn't often see much snow in winter and if we did it didn't stay around very long, so I took every opportunity, while it lasted, to get out in it, sledging, making snowmen and joining in snowball fights. Once after an unusually heavy snowfall I was outside my home with a few of my friends and we were having some target practice with snowballs. A man wearing a trilby hat (I have a thing about trilbies that seems to bring out the worst in me) walks by – some of my friends dare me to throw a snowball and try to knock it off his head. Taking up the challenge I chuck a snowball and hit the brim of the hat. It twists sideways on his head but somehow manages to stay on. My friends scarper – the guy turns round and glares before slowly walking towards me – my face is bright red by this time – I'm given a lecture and reprimanded for my stupidity before he walks off with his hat still twisted halfway around his head. It looked so funny, my friends burst into laughter as soon as he was a safe distance away. My sister ran and told my mum what I'd done and she called me in and gave me another lecture before confining me to the house for the rest of the day.

September 1954 arrived and I joined a small group of twelve pupils who were going to study for GCEs. We were only able to take a maximum of three subjects each as there was a limit to the facilities and tutors available at our school. I opted to study English Language, Maths and Biology.

I soon amassed armfuls of textbooks and exercise books and my dad came up with a large canvas satchel – which looked like it came from an army surplus store – for me to carry them in. It was very robust but looked as though it had been through the wash a few times and was a very faded greyish-beige colour. My friends soon took to covering it with rude and amusing comments, although my parents didn't see the funny side. My mother used to give the satchel a good scrub at weekends to get rid of them, but as this just made it more faded – and more tempting to budding scribes – she soon gave up.

The twelve of us who were studying for GCEs were given individual timetables to concentrate on our chosen subjects and dropped most other lessons. We also had a number of free periods for unsupervised study. We had several other privileges and freedoms as well, but were warned not to abuse them, or else! We had to act like adults and be a shining example to the rest of the school.

Along with the other students who were taking biology, I was allowed to use the biology lab during free periods, and this became my base for the next two years. We conducted endless experiments, some linked to our studies, others of more dubious merit. One of my partners in crime was Ken. We decided to make a small steam-powered contraption based on Hero's engine (we got the idea from a science lesson). After heating a glass tube over a Bunsen burner, we blew it into the required shape and suspended it on a piece of wire formed into a hook and inserted into a piece of wood so that it could spin freely. We gently warmed up the glass object so that it would suck up a small amount of water as it cooled; we then hung it on the wire hook and held it over the Bunsen burner where it spun furiously.

After having successfully made a few of these small models, we decided to attempt a much larger version. All went well until, as it was being heated up, it suddenly exploded. I managed to duck in time but, as I surveyed the damage, I noticed, despite Ken's assurances that he was all right, that his face was covered with small scratches. Looking closer, I could see tiny shards of glass sticking out of his skin. The next hour or so I spent gingerly plucking the shards of glass out of his face, using some tweezers I managed to borrow from one of the girls. It was a miracle none went into his eyes. We were both lucky to escape relatively unscathed from this foolhardy experiment – it certainly taught us an important lesson.

Studying for GCEs brought many new challenges. Maths was my best subject, but even here I struggled to come to grips with geometry. Dave, a mate of mine who lived a few doors away, was also taking GCE Maths and we spent many hours

On the beach age 15 – look at the new haircut as fashion and appearance begin to be important

in the evenings and at weekends trying to master its complexities. Although we generally managed to understand the theories, solving the tests to prove them was another thing entirely. Try as we might, we just didn't seem to be able to work them out. In desperation we decided to take the most difficult ones (marked with asterisks in our textbook) and keep trying again and again, together and separately, until we arrived at the correct answers. Eventually we managed to crack a few of them and soon the mysteries of geometry began to unravel.

English, though, was a different story. I was miles behind the others and not making any real progress. The problem was that I lacked many of the basics, which simply hadn't been covered in the B stream. My essays were poor – maybe I lacked imagination. Unfortunately, nobody seems to have realised this or suggested additional tuition to try to help. There was another problem as well, which my English teacher outlined to my mum and dad at a parents' evening – she found it hard to discipline me and make me knuckle down because I had 'such a lovely smile'. She just couldn't bring herself to read me the riot act – I just made her crumble and feel sorry for me. My mum told her that I used my smile to get away with everything and that she should ignore it. From then on, my English teacher regularly instructed me to 'stop smiling', which of course I did. My mum had warned me that if my performance in English didn't improve I'd have to leave school, so this was an added incentive to try and make sense of a subject I seemed to have little affinity for.

As Christmas approached we put up decorations in the biology lab. The girls in the group did most of the work, but I decided there should be mistletoe. The question was where to put it? The biology lab was long and narrow, and I came up with the idea of a pulley system stretching the length of the room, so that by pulling a string at either end the mistletoe could be moved up and down and manoeuvred to most parts of the room. When one of the girls came into the lab it just took a quick pull on the string followed by a 'look up there' to get a kiss under the mistletoe. It was great fun and we had few refusals. Our enterprise was generally well received: on one occasion when Mr Barber, the biology teacher, caught me in a clinch with one of the girls he just said, 'Go on Wally!' – the nickname I was known by at the time – turned on his heel and left the room.

When we returned to school in January 1955 we were told that some of us wouldn't be able to take our GCEs the following year because we wouldn't be old enough. We were then split into two groups of six. I was one of those held back a year, while Dave went into the other group. This was a blow, because we had helped each other with our homework and had worked well together. Now we would have to work independently.

Derek, a good mate and one of the other boys in my class but not in the GCE group, sat next to me for morning and afternoon registration. One afternoon, while the register was being checked after lunch, he sat at his desk taking sips from a small bottle. I happened to know, having sampled it earlier, that it contained whisky diluted with water. When we left the classroom to go to our first lesson Derek walked out taking a swig from the bottle.

'What's in that bottle?' the form mistress asked him.

He could have said anything – we were gobsmacked when he replied honestly, 'only dilute whisky, miss'.

He was told to stay behind as we went off to our lesson. It was almost over before Derek walked in accompanied by a very cross headmaster. Stopping the lesson, he held up the bottle.

'Stand up if you have had any of this.'

I stood up, along with ten others.

'Come with me', he ordered, and we trooped off behind him to his office. There each of us was called in individually while the rest waited outside. He told us that we had all committed a very serious offence: he would be writing to our parents and we faced expulsion. We were each given six strokes of the cane on both hands, had our names recorded in a book and were sent back to our lessons. We all worried about when the letter would arrive. The next two or three weeks seemed endless as we waited for the fateful day – but it never came. None of us, I am sure, has ever forgotten this incident, nor how much worse the outcome could have been. Looking back, I still think we were very lucky to have been treated so leniently. Strength in numbers, perhaps?

On 12 January 1956 I was admitted to the men's ward of the Bath & Wessex Orthopaedic Hospital for three days. I had now been in every ward in the hospital – including the girls' ward! I wonder how many other patients can claim this rather dubious distinction? This time, though, I wouldn't be receiving treatment. I'd been asked to attend by Mr Price, who was holding a seminar for doctors and orthopaedic surgeons. I was one of several polio victims he wanted to appear to show the progress made following my various operations and treatments. The seminar was spread over two days and was attended by about 50 people. Each patient was shown into a small cubicle, undressed and fitted with a fig leaf, so that that he could be fully examined. There were two reasons Mr Price particularly wanted me to attend: first, the difference in the length of my legs was now down to less than a quarter of an inch; second, given the weakness of my left leg, my ability to walk without a calliper was astonishing. The medical team showed great interest in me, and Mr.

Price was obviously proud of the progress I'd made under his supervision. At the end of the second day, as the seminar was drawing to a close, I had to walk, wearing only my shorts, up and down the room in front of about 50 people as Mr Price explained about me and the excellent progress I had made. It was a very interesting experience and I was honoured to be asked to attend.

The letter from Mr Price asking me to attend the seminar at the hospital

One of the girls in my new GCE group was Molly. She was studying the same subjects as me and over the two years leading up to our exams we became inseparable, working and studying together both in and out of school and helping each other to improve our marks. When we took our mock exams, a month or so before the GCEs, we were delighted to find that we both stood a good chance of passing all three subjects.

Then came the exams proper. We both felt fairly relaxed about the whole procedure and reasonably confident that we'd done OK. All we could do now was to wait for the results. In the meantime came my last Speech Day at Oakfield School. In previous years I'd received a progress prize and a few small awards, but this time I was to be awarded the coveted Public Spirit Cup – a real honour. A few days before the ceremony Mr Ward called me into his office to tell me how thrilled he was that I had been nominated. Not only that: for the first time in the history of the cup there'd been only one nomination; the teachers had agreed unanimously that it should go to me. When I went up on stage in front of the whole school I felt so proud. I was not at all concerned about my limp, everyone knew I had it, and it had made no difference. The claps and cheers I received were so rewarding – this had been a fantastic journey that had ended so much better than I could have ever thought possible. I am so indebted to the teachers who helped me after a very troubled and weak start to my school career – and in particular to my outstanding teacher, friend and confidant Mr Ward. I am also so thankful that my mum and dad, along with my brother and sister, encouraged and supported me so unselfishly.

My final school report also contained comments that stand as a permanent reminder of my achievements at Oakfield School:

'His cheerfulness is a tonic to us all. I have a very high opinion of this boy.'
Mr Hobby, Headmaster

'A boy for whom I have the greatest of respect and admiration.'

Mr Barber, Biology Teacher

'One cannot fail to have the greatest admiration for Philip's personal triumph over his physical disability. This spirit, with sustained hard work, could give him quite an advantage over his fellow men.'

Mr Ward, Maths Teacher

A few weeks later I received my examination results – I had passed all three subjects.

CHAPTER NINE

Work and Marriage

Mr Barber, my biology teacher, had arranged for me to see the manager at the local branch of the Westminster Bank for a job interview. I turned up in my best suit looking really spick and span and enthusiastic about starting full-time work. After a few minutes I was shown into a large office, where a friendly-looking man with a grey moustache, cut very short but covering the whole of his upper lip, sat behind a huge desk. He stood up and gave me a firm handshake before asking me to sit down and ordering tea. I had never been into a bank manager's office before and was very impressed – just the kind of job I would like, I thought. I knew very little about banks except that they offered jobs for life with excellent prospects. Mum and dad didn't have a bank account – which was normal for working-class families at the time – but I knew that anyone who worked in a bank needed a mathematical brain.

He told me that I had been recommended to him and had an excellent reference from my school. The interview went really well. I managed to answer all his questions about why I wanted to work in a bank and about my ambitions. He asked me if I would be prepared to study for further qualifications to advance my career; I said I would be more than happy to. The interview over, he took me on a tour of the bank to explain how it worked and introduce me to some of the staff.

When we returned to his office, he told me he would be delighted for me to join the bank as a trainee. I was thrilled. He handed me some books and pamphlets on banking and told me that I would have to attend a medical examination at head office in London before being appointed. Assuring me this should be a mere

*The Westminster Bank on the corner of the
Market Place in Frome*

formality, he shook my hand and said he looked forward to seeing me in a few weeks.

A few days later a letter arrived fixing the day for my medical examination. Dad was eligible for cheap-rate travel because of his job on the railway, so he took the day off work and went up with me to London. On arrival at Paddington we took the underground to Lothbury. Dad knew London well, because of the years he had spent there during the war, and we reached our destination without any difficulty. I really enjoyed the trip and my father's company. We didn't spend a lot of time together because of him working away from home, and the points of interest and stories he shared with me that day were very special to me.

We entered the bank's massive head office where, after a few minutes wait, I was taken to see the Senior Employment Officer. He told me that, subject to a satisfactory medical report, I would be joining the staff of the Frome Branch. I was then taken to see a doctor. He asked me a few questions before sending me back to the waiting room and telling me to wait until I was called. After about twenty minutes, I was summoned into another office where a young official was sitting behind a desk. He wasted no time in getting to the point.

'I'm sorry to tell you but you have failed your medical and we will be unable to employ you.'

I was shocked, disappointed and angry and demanded to see the Senior Employment Officer again. This was duly arranged, although it was made clear that my request was not only unusual but very unwelcome. When I entered his office he was clearly surprised to see me again. He seemed embarrassed and not sure how to handle me. I was determined to stand up for myself and object to what I considered to be a wrong decision. A lengthy discussion took place. I was cross and at one point thumped the desk with my fist. But all he said was, 'we do not think you could physically do the job – we have had staff returning to us after polio and they struggled'.

'I had polio when I was four', I replied, absolutely incensed, 'I do not remember what it was like to have two good legs – I've grown up with it – contact my school – they will tell you I play football and cricket and join in most things – there is very little I can't do – you don't have to take my word for it!'

It was all to no avail; he refused to change his decision and I left the building upset, disappointed and frustrated at the shortsighted attitude of my prospective employers. Still, it was their loss! My dad was as surprised at the outcome as I was, but offered a sympathetic ear and suggested that I should keep my chin up and try another bank. He also said I should have contacted him before going back to see the Employment Officer as he would gladly have accompanied me to give his support, but this had never entered my head – I was so used to fighting my own battles. We said little on the way back to Frome; we were both pondering what to do for the future. When we arrived home mum shared our disappointment, but comforted me and agreed with dad that I should try another bank. I was not too worried about this setback. I was still annoyed at their stupid decision, but confident I would soon have a job, and even more determined to secure one.

Undeterred, I obtained application forms from the other four high street banks, completed them and posted them off. All the application forms asked the same question – 'have you applied to any other bank – if so which one?' I considered not mentioning my interview with the Westminster Bank, but thought it best to be completely honest. Within a short time I received the same reply from all four banks: 'We regret to inform you that your application has been unsuccessful'. I had no interviews or any other form of communication – just a point-blank refusal. It was obvious that they had all contacted the Westminster to find out why I had been turned down. I had no chance to present myself for consideration or medical examination, and this seemed grossly unfair.

This is when I came to realise that if you have a disability you have to be better than the average applicant for a job. You have to really impress and stand out, or you will be overlooked. You must really sell and promote yourself! This is especially the case where applicants have little or no experience. Getting the break is critical as experience and knowledge speak volumes about one's ability, and an employer then feels more comfortable and confident in making a job offer. There is discrimination against the disabled, but most people are unwilling to admit it. Personally, I feel that I may also have suffered from an image problem; I can't prove it, but I know that, apart from the muscular problem in my left leg, my general health had always been excellent, and will never be convinced that my limp was the only thing holding me back. I didn't go to grammar school and only had the minimum educational requirements, and this probably counted against me as well. The most encouraging part of this unfortunate debacle was that the local bank manager believed in me. He actually wrote to tell me how sorry he was to hear that I could not take up his job offer, and wished me every success in the future.

Now that I couldn't go into banking I needed to consider an alternative career. I had several interviews with the Youth Employment Officer where we discussed various possibilities including the civil service, accountancy and other clerical jobs. As there was a shortage of suitable vacancies, however, he advised me to apply for a job in the accounts department of a local factory to earn a wage and gain some useful work experience until something more suitable came along. An interview was arranged with the company secretary at Wallington & Weston, part of the Marley Group of Companies, and I was offered a job as clerical assistant in the accounts department with a weekly wage of £4. At the time,

I was still doing my morning paper round and this brought in an extra ten shillings a week.

After about six months Frome Rural District Council advertised for a junior trainee. I made enquiries about what the job entailed and thought it seemed an ideal opportunity. The work sounded interesting, with a good pension, financial assistance towards training and promotion prospects. The successful applicant would work in several departments to find out about the range of the council's activities before specialising in an area they had a particular aptitude for.

I applied for the job and was interviewed by the staff committee of the council, which consisted of about eight councillors. The interview took place in the council chamber, an imposing room with deep carpets, leather chairs and polished tables arranged in a U shape. The chairman sat at the head in a huge ornate chair, and I sat immediately in front of him. The other councillors sat on either side, and from where I sat I could only see the chairman and the Clerk of the Council, who sat by his side. The chairman greeted me with a smile before inviting the members of the committee to ask questions. As I couldn't see them, this was somewhat daunting, but, as none of the questions was that tricky, I soon relaxed and gave what I considered sensible answers. Finally, I was asked if I could do typewriting and shorthand, to which I replied, 'no'.

'It would be useful if you could do shorthand, type and also learn bookkeeping', said the Clerk of the Council. 'Are you prepared to study all three, because they are important?'

'Yes', I replied.

He thanked me and told me I would receive a letter informing me of the outcome of the interview shortly.

I was appointed junior clerk in March 1958 on a starting salary of £200 a year. Initially I worked in the Clerk of the Council's Department in the mornings and the Housing and Building Surveyor's Department in the afternoons.

The council offices where I started my first job

The Clerk of the Council's Department dealt with the legal and committee work of the council, and I was soon involved in correspondence, sending out agendas and minutes, and filing and keeping records. I was also given the job of reorganising the strong room – a large walk-in safe, where agreements, insurance policies, mortgage deeds and other important documents were stored for safe keeping. Everything had to be recorded in ledgers, and all packages and files identified and numbered, so that they could be found when needed.

Once I had done this I was given the responsibility of ensuring that all the council's insurance policies were renewed on time. It was very important that none was overlooked and, as policies came up for renewal every few days, this was an enormous responsibility. I decided to call in the insurance personnel to advise me. I had thought of a possible way to simplify procedures and wanted to know if I could implement it: the council year started on the first of April and my idea was that all policies would be renewed on this date. This would mean that, instead of regularly checking renewals every couple of days, they could be checked just once a year, a less risky and more efficient plan. They told me that all I had to do was change the renewal dates to the first of April and pay a proportional premium on each policy for the current year. As this would virtually halve the insurance premiums payable in the current financial year, it would represent a huge one-off saving for the council. When I took my proposal to the Clerk of the Council and the Chief

Financial Officer, they were absolutely delighted, and amazed that no one had ever thought of such a simple solution before – and me only a spotty-faced 17-year-old office junior! This marked the beginning of my interest in the insurance industry.

The evening classes in typewriting, shorthand and bookkeeping brought more benefits than I'd bargained for. Although there were more young men than girls in the bookkeeping class, I was the only male student in the typewriting and shorthand classes. I really enjoyed being in the company of so many attractive young ladies and, with no competition, soon had several dates. A couple of the friendships became steady for several months. I discovered that the girls became more friendly and interested if you had a girlfriend! I also managed to reach a good commercial standard in all three subjects and passed the exams easily.

Although I had already had several girlfriends, this opportunity to meet more girls reminded me of a discussion we had had in a biology class at school. We were discussing how relationships developed between boys and girls and our biology teacher said it was important to have experience of several different partners if we wanted a long and happy marriage. He explained that if we had several girlfriends we would subconsciously build a mental picture of our ideal partner. Whether he was right only time would tell, but it made sense to me and I was quite happy to give it a try. It seemed the perfect practical experiment – and it wasn't even my idea!

As soon as I was proficient in shorthand and typing I started attending council and committee meetings with the Clerk of the Council to take notes and produce minutes. My duties also included preparing agendas and writing letters.

On 29 November 1961 I was at a dance with my mate Roy when I spotted an attractive blonde girl I hadn't seen before. I knew she must be new to the area and said to Roy, 'see that blonde girl over there – I'm going to take her home tonight'. We both agreed she looked very nice and I thought she was the type of girl I would like to marry – she fitted that mental image my biology teacher had spoken of! Was this love at first sight?

My first plan was to try and get a smile from her, which I soon managed. She was with another girl and I could see that they were chatting and smiling between themselves. I was confident that my early advances had met with success. My next move was to have a dance or two with her before the end of the evening. As it was already late I had to move quickly. I knew from experience that I needed to get to talk to her before she realised I had a limp. Although I found no problem with dating girls who already knew me, girls who didn't were more cautious if they saw me limping. By walking slowly around the edge of the hall I was able to approach her without her being aware of my disability. I found out her name was Christine and we chatted and had a couple of dances before she agreed to let me walk her home.

She lived only a few hundred yards from the hall so we didn't have long together before she was back home. As we set off, she noticed for the first time that I had a limp.

'Have you hurt your leg playing football?' she asked.

'No', I replied, 'I had polio when I was four'. Although it would have been easy to say yes, it never even occurred to me to lie. I believe this was the moment we first trusted each other. I felt confident that Christine felt comfortable with me, and I was surprisingly relaxed with her. I was perfectly happy to talk openly about my disability; it never entered my head that I would be rejected. Was I over confident? I don't really know, but I knew I had to be completely open and honest; it would have been pointless trying to explain things away at a later date.

It simply isn't in my nature to shirk questions about my affliction. I never have and probably never will; it is an integral part of me. I live with it because I have no alternative – and I also have no alternative but to defend myself against those who would do me down. I cannot and will not back off because that is how I am. I have an overwhelming desire to be treated as a normal person and have always striven to achieve this; I could be 'Phil the cripple' or 'Phil with a limp' or just 'Phil' – the difference is massive! Most of my friends and the people I know really well often say they never even notice or think about my limp – to them I am just 'Phil'. I cherish that, to me that is the prize!

Christine had recently moved down from Selly Oak in Birmingham with her parents, who had bought a footwear shop at Badcox in Frome. She lived over the shop and, after a brief chat in the doorway, agreed to come with me to a birthday bash in a local café the following Saturday. The party would go on till midnight and as Christine normally had to be home by 10.30 she would have

Christine and me a few weeks after meeting, at Longleat House in our first photo together

to try to get a 'late pass' if we were to stay till the end.

Saturday arrived and I called at the shop to collect her – surprise, surprise, she wasn't ready. Her mother opened the door and said something like, 'you must be Philip, come on up – she won't be long', and I followed her upstairs to the flat above the shop to meet her father and her brother, Michael.

It must have been twenty minutes or so before she was ready, so her parents had plenty of time to sit and chat to me. This was obviously a ploy to see what I was like and whether I was a suitable boyfriend. I must have passed the test because we were given the 'all clear' to attend the birthday party and stay to the end.

The party and the first date went well and Christine and I soon became inseparable. We fell in love and were engaged on the anniversary of our first meeting, planning to get married within two or three years.

I wanted to buy a house to live in after we were married and one came up for sale near my parents. It was rented out to a couple in their eighties who had a controlled tenancy. This meant that they couldn't be given notice to quit and rent increases were restricted by law. However, they were both frail and didn't plan to stay there much longer. The property was to be sold by auction and was expected to fetch only around half what it would have sold for if it had had vacant possession. It seemed a good idea to try and buy it, as the rent would pay the loan interest. My bank manager agreed to an overdraft up to a maximum of £1000 to fund the purchase if I was successful at the auction, on condition that I contributed £100 towards the transaction. On the day I requested the overdraft I only had a little over £9 in my bank account. Was that cheeky? I did not think so as I was confident in my presentation, and he believed in me – I would soon be a property investor.

Jim, the housing and building surveyor I worked for at the

Our first house, bought at auction for £910 - although we never lived there!

council came to the auction with me. He had looked at the house before the auction and confirmed it was a good sound building in need of some modernisation, and thought it would sell for between £800 and £900. He also agreed to loan me 10% of the accepted bid. I had never been to an auction before, and, after several people had dropped out, I nervously entered the bidding at £750. It increased by £25 at a time and was soon up to £900 against me. Jim then bid £910, the auctioneer announced a new bidder and, as there were no further bids, brought his hammer down. The house was mine. The paperwork was completed and Jim handed over a cheque for £91. I am ever grateful for his support and guidance.

Mr Ward had been an inspiration to me, and I liked to maintain contact with him. I occasionally met him for a pint in his local pub and chatted about my school years. They were always very frank and open discussions. He once told me he remembered me as a small boy being pushed by my mum in an invalid chair past his house. On one occasion he'd said to his wife, 'I hope I teach that boy one day'. I'm so glad he got his wish!

My relationship with some of the other teachers at my school had been less than happy. I found the headmaster particularly difficult to deal with. He praised me in public, but in private his attitude was very different. Years of putting up with this came to a head one day when I was in the bank paying in my monthly pay cheque. I was standing in a long queue – the bank was full – when there was a tap on my shoulder followed by the remark, 'been in trouble with the police lately?' It was my former headmaster.

I was astounded and furious at this remark, and turning to him replied angrily, 'no, I haven't, nor am I ever likely to be – I resent that remark – you are no longer my headmaster – if you cannot speak to me without insulting me don't bother'.

With that I turned my back on him. I'm not sure what effect this had on the rest of the customers in the crowded bank, but I wasn't going to have my character besmirched by insults like that. I think I'd made my point – I don't recall having any trouble from him again.

I have often wondered why my headmaster treated me in this way: praise in public and snide remarks in private – I couldn't understand it. I've discussed it with several of my former teachers and friends and they all say the same thing: 'he felt challenged and was probably afraid of your strong spirit, so he tried to bully you – in effect he was afraid of you'. If that was the reason he had no chance of winning – I just find it incredible that he wanted to try.

I had no immediate prospect of promotion at Frome Rural District Council, so applied for a position as junior committee clerk at Wiltshire County Council in Trowbridge. My application was successful. I was on a higher salary straight away, and, as this rose by annual increments, I worked out that, by the time Christine and I were married, I would be taking home £65 a month. With a mortgage of around £10 a month and a weekly shopping bill of £4 to £5 this would not only meet all our needs but also enable us to save for the future. Although Trowbridge was about eight miles away and I didn't drive, there was a good bus and train service, and several people with cars also made the journey daily.

My time in the Clerk of the County Council's Department at Trowbridge was not a happy one. I couldn't really settle into the work and the atmosphere was much less friendly than at Frome. There was only one other person – my supervisor – in the same office as me, while my line manager worked in an office nearby. Both were very unhelpful, leaving me to struggle along as best I could. I liked to be on top of my job and decided I had to move to another department. Vacancies were advertised internally and, because of the experience I had gained at Frome, I felt qualified to apply for quite a few of them. Several came with higher salaries – an important consideration with my marriage coming up – and I had several interviews, most of which seemed to go well, but with no success. This worried me; I knew I had the right qualifications and on several occasions the office grapevine put me as the front runner. Yet despite all this, I got nowhere. I began to wonder whether, yet again, I was the victim of prejudice.

The Chief Clerk in the Clerk of the Council's Department was an ex-military man and a hard disciplinarian. He could also be very rude and was given to making personal remarks. You had little chance of getting on unless you were one of his favourites – and I never was. He made this quite clear. One day I was walking past his office and the door was open.

'Whitmarsh, come here', he ordered in his booming voice.

'Yes, sir', I replied, walking into his office.

I was then met with this outrageous insult: 'you strike me as being a typical Wiltshire man – bone idle!'

'I was born in Somerset', I replied indignantly, 'I suggest you get your facts right – I resent that remark!' and with that turned on my heel and walked out.

'Come back', he shouted, 'I haven't finished', but I had no intention of going back to be insulted. No one spoke to me like that! Surprisingly, he didn't come after me.

I returned to my office extremely cross. The colleague who'd replaced my previous supervisor, and had become a good friend, tried to calm me down – but I was in no mood to listen. I fully anticipated disciplinary action, but strangely there were no repercussions of any kind – nor do I recall any other unpleasant encounters with this man. Was I vindicated? I believe I was. This incident made me even more determined to move to another department. It was obvious I didn't fit in and if I stayed where I was my prospects were nil.

It wasn't long, however, before I moved, with the support of my new supervisor, to a higher-grade position in the Architect's Department. I was in a team of six, looking after repairs to schools and dealing with architects, building inspectors, engineers and surveyors. My experience in the Housing and Building Surveyor's Office in Frome stood me in good stead and I soon felt on top of the work. It was much better than working in a small office with only one other person, and it was a really happy team.

In the autumn of 1964, about six months before our wedding, we bought 53 Wingfield Road, Trowbridge, as we felt it sensible to live nearer my work. The house in Frome was still rented out and the rental income paid the bank loan. The house in Trowbridge cost £1,400. We put down a £200 deposit and arranged a mortgage at six-and-a-quarter percent, with monthly payments of £9.3s.4d (£9.17). The mortgage was restricted to fifteen years because of the age of the property, which was normal. It was a mid-terrace Victorian house and had two bedrooms, lounge, dining room, kitchen, bathroom, a small front garden and a good-sized rear garden, no garage and no central heating. We repaired, decorated and carpeted it throughout, with some useful assistance from my dad, and finished with a nice cosy house.

Christine applied for a typing job at County Hall in Trowbridge and was offered a position in the Civil Defence Department. She started there a few months before our wedding, so for a time we were both travelling from Frome every day to work.

On Easter Monday, 19 April 1965, we were married at Christchurch in Frome. The reception, attended by 160 guests, was at the Mendip Motel. It was a fabulous day for us both. Our best man was Jim, the husband of Christine's cousin; my sister Margaret and Glennis, a friend, were the bridesmaids. After the reception we left for our honeymoon in Jersey with Diane and Ivor, two old friends who had got married on Easter Saturday, with Christine as

one of the bridesmaids. We stayed at the Grand Hotel for a week – a real taste of luxury. We hired a car and travelled most of the island. I still couldn't drive but Ivor had a full licence and we shared the expenses. It was a wonderful holiday, only marred by the return flight, when the plane developed a fault shortly after take-off. We had to wear seatbelts for almost the whole journey, the flight was very slow and we travelled at a very low altitude – it was really scary. When we finally arrived back at the airport we heaved a sigh of relief and vowed never to fly again.

We soon settled down to married life. With two wages coming in we were not only able to live quite well but also to start saving.

The wedding and honeymoon had drained our resources, but we had no loans or overdraft. After about four months we decided we would like a television, as we missed not having one. We decided against buying one, as they were still expensive and unreliable, so we rented one from a local shop, which meant any repair bills would be taken care of. Our food budget was £4.10s (£4.50) a week but we often spent less. A joint of beef cost ten shillings (50p) and a joint of pork seven shillings (35p), each of which was enough for at least two dinners. Christine was good at controlling the food budget and a brilliant homemaker. Apart from the food expenses I handled all other household expenses.

We had only been married a few months when disaster struck. I was walking home from work one evening when I was almost knocked down by a car that had run out of control. Although I managed to get out of the way, I damaged my right knee (my good leg) so badly that I could hardly walk. Somehow I managed to struggle the last few hundred yards home. My local GP referred me to an orthopaedic surgeon at St Martin's Hospital in Bath who told me I had a badly torn cartilage. He could remove it but warned that this entailed a certain degree of risk. I replied that, as I could hardly walk and seemed to have no immediate prospect of recovery without surgery, I was prepared to take the risk. I had every confidence in him.

Most of the patients in the ward I was admitted to were young men with sporting injuries. I was told by one of the 'hard men' on the ward that the operation to remove a cartilage was very painful and I would really suffer. I said nothing and bided my time – I would deal with him in my own way. A few hours after surgery a physiotherapist came to see me. She asked how I was feeling and if I felt up to a few exercises. I said I was fine and, when she asked me to lift my leg, I found I could do so easily and without any fuss or pain. The face of the 'hard man' was a picture. When the physiotherapist left, he came over to my bed in amazement and I told him of all the operations I'd had in the past – this one was chicken feed – having a tooth out was more painful! That put him in his place. What I didn't tell him was that because my leg was so strong, through having to do the work of two, it made my prospects much better. I had also been on a programme of special exercises to ensure maximum muscle strength, avoiding any wasting through inactivity, before surgery. Within a few weeks I'd made a full recovery and was walking normally again.

We decided it was time for me to take driving lessons, as we were planning to have children and a car would make life much easier. My only concern was that I wouldn't be able to drive a conventional car but would need to have special controls fitted. I contacted Larry, a local driving instructor, who advised me to try to drive a normal car and pass my test in one so that I wouldn't be restricted in the future as to the vehicle I drove. I was confident that, despite the severe muscular weakness in my left leg, I could safely operate the clutch controls. I had sat in many cars and knew I could press the clutch pedal without difficulty. My only problem was lifting my foot onto and off the pedal. Larry watched me as I sat in his car and tried the clutch pedal and told me he was satisfied he could teach me to drive.

Although I had to use one of my hands to help me lift my foot onto the pedal, I could lift it off unaided and Larry considered this was fine. We worked very hard on all aspects of clutch control. I had to practise moving off on the flat without increasing the engine revs or using the accelerator until I could do it without ever stalling the engine. After about eight lessons he told me I was his star pupil and said I was ready for my test.

The fateful day arrived. The examiner was notified of my disability but told me to drive normally and not concern myself about my affliction. The test went well and he asked me to do two three-point-turns to demonstrate my clutch control. These too went without a hitch and I passed.

On the day of Christine's 21st birthday on 30 June 1966, she found out she was pregnant. She also received £50 from a trust fund set up to hold a compensation payment for injuries she received in a car accident when she was 14. What a wonderful day that was! Adding the extra cash to our savings we bought our first car, a dark green Morris Minor, for £125.

During the 1966 World Cup, Christine had to endure lots of football, both on the television and in her tummy! We laughed and joked about whether our first child would be a footballer, although we had no idea whether it was a boy or a girl. England won the World Cup and Kevin Charles was born on 2 December 1966 in Trowbridge Hospital. That was a good year. I was 26 years old and we had our first son – we wanted more children but had agreed that we would try to complete our family before my 30th birthday.

We missed Frome and did not really settle in Trowbridge. Most of our friends and family still lived in Frome and we spent much of our spare time there. Now that we had started a family, we also wanted to move to a bigger house. I was keeping my eye out for job vacancies and one came up that seemed to offer the solution to all our problems – Frome Rural District Council wanted a senior committee clerk. Not only was the salary more than I was getting in Trowbridge, financial assistance was also available towards the cost of moving. My experience fitted me ideally for the post and my application was successful. We sold our house in Trowbridge and moved back to Frome, where we stayed with Christine's parents for a few months while we waited for our new bungalow to be built.

In the spring of 1968 we moved into 14 Wythburn Road in Frome. This had three bedrooms, lounge/diner, kitchen, bathroom, central heating, garage, a good-sized front garden and a large rear garden with open views. The purchase price was £3,590 and, as we had some equity from the sale of our previous house, we arranged a mortgage with the Council for £3,000 over 25 years. We now had a really nice family home, in a nice quiet cul-de-sac, absolutely ideal for children.

CHAPTER TEN

Moving On: Bridgwater, Hastings and Kent

My prospects in the local government service seemed slim unless I continually moved to new councils. There seemed little chance of in-house promotion at Frome for the foreseeable future as most of the staff were relatively young and settled. I had passed several exams and was well qualified, with excellent experience, but I needed a higher salary if I wanted to improve my family's standard of living. I felt that my wife and son deserved better and it was up to me to do something about it. We wanted more children but this would have stretched our resources to the limit. I wanted more control over my income and lifestyle and wasn't prepared to stay where I was in the hope that something would turn up.

I discussed the situation with Christine and convinced her that after 11 years in local government my future lay elsewhere. I wanted a new career where I could use my numeracy skills to their best advantage. Christine supported me and trusted my decision to look for a job in insurance. I had a general knowledge of insurance and felt it was time to specialise. At 28 I considered I could switch successfully to a new career where I would be judged on my results. The future was in my hands. Giving up a safe job with a good pension was a risk, of course, as many of my friends and family were quick to point out. My dad, in particular, was totally opposed to the idea; he became angry when I told him of my plans and eventually refused to discuss them at all. He told me I should look after the job I'd got and not throw it all away, but taking the soft option was never my style and I stuck to my guns.

After discussions with various insurance companies and people I knew in the industry I decided to join the London &

Manchester Insurance Company as an agent. I liked the manager, who was only a few years older than me, and had left a job in a bank to join the company. He had been promoted to manager within a very short space of time and this confirmed my opinion that, with hard work, the rewards were there for the taking. I had my sights set on becoming a manager and was convinced I could make it. I was in control of my destiny – in total contrast to my time in local government. The only downside was that my starting salary was about £500 a year less than I was currently earning – but I was confident that I could earn sufficient commission not only to make up the difference but to come out with even more. If I couldn't, then I would have to admit that I had made a mistake, but I had absolute confidence that I would be successful in my new career and was eager to start.

I was anxious, however, after my disastrous experiences with the banking industry, to get medical clearance before I started my new job. The banking and insurance industries had similar rules, with non-contributory pension schemes which had medical conditions and requirements. The Manager told me that a medical examination would be arranged after I had completed a six-month probationary period, but I insisted this was done right away. I simply couldn't take the risk of being dismissed on medical grounds six months down the line, so arrangements were made for me to see my GP, Dr Begley, who was conversant with my health and disability. He gave me a full check-up, discussed the physical demands of the work and produced a report for my new employer stating that, in his opinion, I was capable of doing the job.

I started work for the London & Manchester in August 1968. The manager spent the first two weeks training me in all aspects of the business. My main duties were to collect premiums, sell new policies, and maintain accurate cash accounts. Weekly premiums were recorded in a collecting book, while monthly, quarterly and yearly premiums were recorded on a collection return. Collections were an important part of the job, as weekly premiums had to be maintained at a high percentage (96% or better). This paid my basic salary, with all other collections paying a commission once they had gone through the accounts. Sales of new policies paid good commissions, although if they lapsed within a short time the commissions had to be refunded – or, in insurance jargon, clawed back. Honesty, good knowledge of the products and rapport with clients were all vital for success.

My first few weeks went well and I was soon competent in all aspects of the work. My mathematical ability was an enormous help; I found cash-collecting duties easy and had no problem keeping cash records. Because I was quick on the accounts side, I had more time to spend on selling – the real income-generating side of the business. Before joining the company I had established that, although the basic salary was lower than that offered by many other companies, the commission rates were significantly higher. I considered this to my advantage, as it allowed me to dictate my own income. In a way it was like running my own business – another ambition of mine.

By the end of November, just over two months after joining the team, I was the top new business producer in the Frome Office. I was also rated highly in the South West Division. All the other agents in Frome had started at the beginning of the year – I was the only one that had joined later. My progress was noted by the senior management, no doubt prompted by Grant Cowley, my manager, who had said I was promotion material from the start. My dad was also much happier now that my change of job had proved successful – it was no longer a taboo subject between us.

Mr Thew, the Divisional Manager from Bristol, made an appointment to see me in the Frome Branch Office to discuss my future career. Grant had told me that he would be offering me promotion, either to Divisional Assistant (Trainee Manager) or Industrial Branch Life Inspector. He advised me to take the Life Inspector's position as it would help me develop my selling skills and would earn me more money. He advised me against the

Divisional Assistant's job, which he described as a 'dogsbody of a job' with little opportunity to enhance my earnings. It would also entail being sent almost anywhere in the South West at short notice, and, although it was supposed to be a trainee manager's post, I could be in for a long wait before I became a manager. In his opinion, I should stick to selling because I was good at it. If I had a proven record as a salesman my future would be bright; furthermore all promotions carried salary enhancements, so the more I earned the better it would be for future basic salary negotiations.

Grant introduced me to the Divisional Manager before leaving me alone with him in his office. He told me how pleased he was with my performance and how well I had done in a very short time. He thought I should be rewarded for my efforts. Then the interview took an unexpected turn for the worse. The personnel department had advised him that, because of my disability, I would be unable to join the company pension scheme. I was shocked and replied, 'this is ridiculous. I had a medical check-up before I joined to avoid such stupidity – but if that's the case I won't join the scheme – I'll do the job without a pension'.

Mr Thew laughed, threw his papers on the floor and stood up to shake my hand vigorously.

'That's what I like', he replied, 'someone with spirit and determination – you will go far. Let's talk about this promotion'.

'The quicker the better – when I am promoted I will be a company official and automatically become a member of the pension scheme, so this rubbish about not being fit enough to do the job will no longer apply.'

'You understand the rules better that I do', was his somewhat amused response, 'I can see you as a branch manager quite soon'.

We discussed my promotion prospects. He explained the pros and cons of the two jobs on offer. We agreed that the insurance business needed managers who could sell so that they could train and assist others to be successful. Producing regular new business was the key to the growth of the company. He then offered me promotion to Life Inspector (Industrial Branch), which would allow me to specialise in selling and promoting weekly premiums for life insurance and savings plans. I would work with agents across the South West, assisting them to write new business with their customers by working a week at a time with them on planned programmes. Finally we agreed that my longer-term objective would be to manage a branch within a relatively short timescale, provided I continued to do well and proved my ability to encourage other members of staff to improve and generate good sales. It was team effort that was needed and it was up to me to promote it. In essence this arrangement meant that, although I was not being promoted to a recognised trainee manager post, I was earmarked as a future branch manager.

In January 1969, after five months working as an agent, I started my new job as a Life Inspector. My main obstacle was that many agents did not like working with inspectors. Many of them felt that the commission structure did not encourage them to write new business assisted by officials like me; this was because 'unassisted business' (submitted by an agent personally) carried higher commissions than 'assisted business'. Many inspectors also had the reputation of not helping agents produce new business; they simply milked agents' best prospects, closing sales on agents' known prospects and requiring them to work even harder to generate new business. This meant I had constantly to overcome agents' prejudices against inspectors. For many of them, it was something of a culture shock; I genuinely wanted to help them build a successful business and earn more money. I didn't want to steal their easy business; I wanted to help them find genuine new sales and produce more opportunities in areas they found difficult or had overlooked. Many agents, for example, became too familiar with their customers and found it difficult to seek more business from them.

Many inspectors only wanted the 'cream' and refused to work with agents who had a poor track record. I, on the other hand, was prepared to work with agents irrespective of whether they were good bad or indifferent, and generate additional income for both of us. I wanted to build common respect and partnership, and was confident that, once I had worked with an agent, he would want to work with me again and give me his full co-operation.

This was not an easy strategy, but gradually it started to produce results and I was soon writing good levels of new business with very low lapse rates. Good quality business meant more income, and no commission refunds. Word soon spread that my approach was different and I found that I was welcomed rather than resented when I turned up on a new patch. Agents suddenly wanted to work with me, my approach had paid off and, even though I often worked in branches that were performing below par, my sales figures were excellent and I was up with the best in the division very quickly. As yet I hadn't been to Plymouth or Gloucester – regarded as the best offices in the South West, and where inspectors went to boost their confidence if they were going through a bad patch. In many ways I did not have an easy start, but although it was perhaps unfair, things could only improve. It also proved to me that I could generate business anywhere, and with anyone.

I had been in my new job about a year when I ran into the Vice Chairman of Frome Rural District Council in the town centre. He asked me how things were going and told me that the council missed me. I told him I had already been promoted and my prospects looked good. I also told him that my main reason for leaving the council was that I'd needed to boost my income to improve my family's standard of living. At the council, I had been on around £1,000 a year; twelve months into my new job I was earning around £2,000. We parted on good terms and he said that if my circumstances ever changed he would welcome me back.

Kevin was now almost four years old and, with my salary double what it had been, we could afford to have another child. Justin James was born at Frome Victoria Hospital on 22 August 1970. I'd always wanted our children to be born before I was 30, and, as my thirtieth birthday was just over two months away, it was a fairly close run thing.

Unfortunately, my success had some unpleasant repercussions. Word began to filter back to me that people were making remarks such as 'it won't last', 'I don't believe it', 'what's the catch', 'he must be writing rubbish', 'he must be telling lies' or 'he's getting all the cream'. I couldn't believe this was happening – it seemed unreal. It was disturbing that anyone could be so untruthful, unkind and vindictive, but I came to realise there is something odd about being successful, and even more so if you have a disability. People are only too ready to knock you. A disability also brings another odd reaction in that when you take someone able-bodied on at his or her own game and beat them, they withdraw all help and start finding excuses for your success, often resorting to exaggerations and untruths.

I was working in Bristol and, for some reason, had a poor production week. As Mr Thew worked in the same building, I knew he would want to see me and, sure enough, he left an urgent message for me to come to his office. After shaking hands and exchanging a few pleasantries, he came to the point.

'What went wrong last week?'

Truthfully, confidently – but perhaps with an element of cheek – I replied, 'if I knew that, I wouldn't have had a bad week!'

He laughed and replied, 'that's a new one – I will accept it this time – but don't use it again!'

We then had a chat about how I was finding the new job and how Christine and the boys were getting on. He was a superb motivator; rather like Mr. Ward he changed my life dramatically, and after twenty minutes or so I felt ten foot tall. He always inspired and encouraged me and I had the greatest admiration and respect for him. He took me for lunch and we chatted about my future and what he could do to help, and he told me how pleased he was with my progress. He said he would do anything he could to further my career. This was my opportunity to tell him how unfair I thought the programming of inspectors was. I told him I wasn't getting a fair crack of the whip, being sent to small offices all the time rather than the larger offices where there were more opportunities. He accepted what I said and promised it would be rectified, and it was. He was, as always, very much a man of his word.

Shortly after this I was sent to the Plymouth Office for four weeks. This was my first visit to what was considered the best branch in the division. Unusually the manager worked with me for the first few days and we had a very productive time. After the second day he invited me to a pub for a pint.

'I've enjoyed working with you', he said, 'I had heard you were straight and honest – you are'.

I smiled and said, 'there is no point in selling rubbish. It proves nothing, and if you tell the truth you don't have to remember what you said!'

We then discussed the programme for the rest of my visit, and he told me he was confident I would do well and get on with the staff. I had a brilliant four weeks at Plymouth and, when I left, the manager and many of the staff told me I would be welcome there any time. After this, the rumours and lies that had been spread about me dried up. I had won the battle by sticking to my principles. I was accepted as being on a par with the other inspectors and given a fairer schedule, with visits to larger offices alternating with spells in the smaller ones. My production levels remained consistently high. Amazingly, one inspector, who had been top producer for many years, found he at last had some real competition and moved to a manager's job, something he'd reputedly sworn he'd never do.

After about three years as an inspector I was promoted to branch manager at Bridgwater in January 1972. This was a new branch formed by splitting the branch at Taunton. It was in Castle Street, a very old part of the town. I knew the area well. The agents were all experienced and good at their jobs; I had worked with them on many occasions and was confident we would make an excellent team.

As Bridgwater was about forty miles from Frome, we put our bungalow up for sale and started house hunting in the Bridgwater area. We soon found a detached bungalow in the village of Moorland, a few miles outside Bridgwater. Orchard View, Moorland, had three large double bedrooms, bathroom, kitchen/diner, lounge, garage/workshop, and a quarter-acre garden. The garden was very overgrown and needed landscaping and the house had no central heating. We estimated it would cost around £1,000 to install central heating and negotiated £1,000 off the asking price. In the end, we paid £7,500 for the bungalow, selling our home in Frome for £6,500. It was in a delightful setting, with access to the M5, then nearing completion, about two miles away. There were also good roads to Frome, Taunton and Bridgwater, a good village school, post office, church and pub.

We moved into our new home about three months after I started my new job. Kevin, who had turned five and was attending Wesley Infants School in Frome – thus maintaining a Whitmarsh family tradition – moved to Moorland School. Justin was just coming up to two. We had the garden landscaped, installed central heating and set about decorating throughout. We soon had a lovely home again. Christine was so good at this and always knew how to create a wonderful home for our two boys and me very quickly – she was brilliant. Consequently we all settled in and made new friends and soon felt as though we had been there for years.

My branch did really well and I had the full support of all my staff. I worked hard to develop a really good team spirit and everyone responded to this. By the end of the first year we had exceeded our targets in all three types of business – Industrial Branch (weekly premiums for life insurance and savings plans), Ordinary Branch (monthly, quarterly, half-yearly and yearly premiums for life insurance and savings plans), and General Branch (all non-life insurance for property, cars, house contents, etc).

At the start of each business week – which fell on a Thursday – I met up with all the agents in the pub, in the evening, to see how

Dinner at the Grand Hotel in Bristol in the company of the chairman, Lewis Whyte, and the managing director, Mr Browne

they'd done and ensure they all had some new business for the coming week. If anyone had a problem then everyone else would try to help out. These were really good social occasions and helped to build an excellent team.

We finished the year as top branch in the South West Division and won the District Cup for best all-round branch for the year. Our results for the year were outstanding: we had increased premium income by 43% – a company record – and were invited to a superb celebration dinner in Bristol as a reward, sitting on the top table with the chairman of the company.

That summer we went on holiday to Pontin's in Paignton. It was good for families with young children as there was so much to do, and if the weather was inclement there was plenty of entertainment. One afternoon, there was a family 'muck about' around the swimming pool and children were encouraged to take part in races across the width of the pool. Without any warning the Bluecoats grabbed several fathers, myself included, and marched

With my nephew Dean at Pontin's

us up to the deep end of the pool. We had been selected to take part in a swimming race. Suddenly, one of the Bluecoats took me aside.

'I'm sorry', he said, 'I hadn't realised you had a bad leg – if you want to quietly go back to your family that's OK'.

'That's all right', I replied confidently, 'I'll beat most of these anyway!'

We lined up, the whistle blew and we all dived in. One bloke was soon out of sight – he must have been a professional. I had no chance of catching him but I was in a scrap for second place, ending up third after being beaten by a fingertip. Most of the others were yards behind and some gave up. I felt quite satisfied with my performance. That evening in the bar, just before the entertainment started, several of the Bluecoats came over, shook me by the hand and said, 'have a drink on us – you were great this afternoon – thanks for being a good sport'. One of them then said how embarrassed he'd been when he realised I had a limp.

'Don't worry about it', I said, 'it turned out all right!' I think I went up in their estimation from that point and we enjoyed much friendly banter and a few pints for the remainder of the holiday. Nice one.

Over the next two years the branch continued to do well and life in Moorland was very pleasant. We had a good social life and became very involved in the local community. The village pub was excellent and I became a member of the skittle team, as well as joining the carnival club. Christine made friends with several young mums and attended many weekly functions. Kevin and Justin had several friends in the village and enjoyed playing in the wonderful country setting of fields and apple orchards – a haven for young children, climbing trees, building dens and fishing.

There was one unpleasant incident shortly after we moved into the village when a boy said to Kevin, 'you've got a funny dad with a funny leg'. This really upset him and he came home to tell me about it. He didn't really know how to fight so I gave him a few lessons. Shortly after this I understand there was a punch up and the insults stopped. A chip off the old block?

After I'd been at Bridgwater for three years, Mr Thew, who'd been promoted to director, approached me about moving to the Hastings branch. As this was a much larger office my basic salary would rise by £1,000 a year and there would be greater opportunities to earn commission. It was a wonderful opportunity, but not only did my divisional manager want me to stay where I was, I didn't want to leave Somerset either, especially as it would mean uprooting my family yet again.

Christine, however, wasn't too happy with my social life – in particular the amount of time I was away from home working or down the pub. Our marriage was for the first time a bit shaky and because of this I thought a move might not be such a bad idea. Frankly, I was being rather selfish and not supporting her in the home enough, and, as she was looking after two young lodgers as well as the children, she had a lot on her plate.

I am not sure what would have happened had we stayed in Bridgwater but the decision was taken out of my hands after a serious argument with my divisional manager. I had been told not to mention my possible move to Hastings to anyone but Christine – it had to be treated in the strictest confidence. Five weeks passed and I received no word about what was happening. I wasn't sure what was causing the delay, but supposed it was to do with negotiations on earnings, terms and salary. Naturally, I was anxious about my future and eventually decided to contact a friend of mine, a former Bristol district manager who had been promoted to divisional manager, to see if he could find out.

Unbeknown to me, this got back to my divisional manager, who summoned me to see him urgently at divisional office.

'Have you been talking to anyone about your move to Hastings?' he asked me angrily when I arrived.

'No', I replied.

He repeated the question twice and I continued to deny it. The fourth time, however, I replied, 'you have asked me this question several times – you obviously know I have spoken to someone – if you had not kept me waiting so long this would not have happened'.

I then received a lecture about honesty, integrity and discretion. He started criticising my work and produced a printout of my results in Bridgwater. I couldn't believe this – after all that had happened, suddenly I was being accused of being a bad manager.

'This is ridiculous', I snapped, pointing to the figures, 'these figures are the ones I discussed with you a few weeks ago – my signature is on the sheet! When we discussed them then you were perfectly happy – no way can they now be that bad – this is unfair and unacceptable.'

A heated exchange followed, which ended with me standing up and walking out, only pausing in the doorway to announce sarcastically, 'I think that was a draw – one all!'

'Come back', he shouted angrily, 'I haven't finished', but I was in no mood to return for more of the same.

I went home and told Christine what had happened.

'Whatever happens now', I said, 'I am going to Hastings – I will never be forgiven for this'.

I had made up my mind, probably for the wrong reasons, that I should move. But I was also ambitious and I wanted to manage a larger branch and, in the longer term perhaps, become a divisional manager.

My staff in Bridgwater were disappointed that I had decided to move on and several of them tried to persuade me to stay. But they realised I had made a decision and would not change it. They arranged a fantastic leaving party for me in Taunton and we had a formal dinner with tremendous support from the whole division – including the divisional manager. Some of them said they had never seen so much support for a leaving-do before and remarked, 'it shows how popular you are'. That was a tremendous moment for me.

When I walked into the dining room with Christine to take my seat there was a huge floor to ceiling banner on the wall with the words 'See Me' on it. I laughed! This had been arranged by my agents in recognition of one of my systems in the office. If I needed to speak to one of them about an important matter, I would write 'see me' on a letter or document, and place it in their personal post box for them to collect when they called into the office. They knew that if they failed to see me promptly they would have a problem, as I wouldn't forget I'd put it there. I don't think they liked the system very much when I first introduced it, but they eventually accepted it and realised it was important to act responsibly when requested to do so. The fact that they made such a joke of it demonstrated that they respected me and accepted that there always have to be basic ground rules. They had also come to recognise that I would always do everything in my power to support them.

The warmth of that occasion is something I will never forget. I realised, for the first time, that I was highly respected and regarded within the company. Many of my colleagues spoke about my qualities and abilities. Significantly, many also said that if my new job did not work out they would be happy to welcome me back. Some of the branch managers said jokingly they were glad I was moving on as I was such a tough opponent.

Some months later, one of my senior agents wrote to me, saying, 'we are glad your new job is going well. We are sorry you went – we did not realise how good it was until you left us – thanks.' Again, something I will never forget.

In the autumn of 1975 I started my new position as branch manager in Hastings. This meant staying away from home all week and returning at weekends. The drive from Moorland to Hastings took about five hours, as there was no direct motorway link.

In the first week at my new office I encountered a few problems. The staff were pleasant to my face but, when they got together in the staff area, it was a different story. What they didn't realise was that, because of the thinness of the walls, I could hear much of what was said. On one occasion, I overheard one of them saying to the others, 'have you seen our new manager – what do you think – have you heard him speak – do you realise he is crippled?'

I could understand my West Country accent being a source of interest and intrigue but felt that the situation needed to be dealt with diplomatically or my position as manager would soon be seriously undermined. I had to act swiftly, so on the first Wednesday – the end of my first business week – I arranged a 'beer and sandwich' bonding session at a local pub, making it compulsory for all agents to attend. I chatted about my plans for the future of the branch and we got to know and understand each other much better. I had identified the speaker of the words I had heard through my office wall, and, as the gathering started to break up, took him quietly to one side and said, 'I might talk slow, but I think flipping fast – got it!'

'I am not sure I know what you mean?' he replied, clearly taken aback.

'Just think about what you have been chatting about in the office since I arrived – I've heard it all', I said – then, having given that time to sink in, added, 'I can be your best friend or your worst enemy – it's up to you!'

The result of this brief encounter was quite amazing. The atmosphere in the office changed almost overnight and there was soon a buzz about the place. I'd made my point and nipped trouble in the bud. Word soon got around that I wouldn't take any messing about or insults, and they realised I was a lot tougher than they first thought. New business production improved dramatically and we were soon one of the best branches in the division. We also had a good team spirit. Most of us met up on Thursday evenings for a pint and a game of snooker. Unlike me, several of the agents were excellent snooker players, and they really enjoyed thrashing the manager. They referred to me as 'eight and tidy' due to my habit of potting a red followed by the black and leaving the white as safe as possible.

After about three months of travelling to Hastings from Bridgwater, we sold our bungalow in Moorland for £14,500 and purchased 3 Henderson Close, Hastings, a detached house with a large lounge, large dining room, four bedrooms, garage and small garden for £16,500. There were excellent walks nearby as well as a lovely park. We had to stay in temporary accommodation for about two months before we could move into our new home, but we were together as a family again. Justin had just turned five and started attending the same school as Kevin.

At the end of my first year, the Hastings branch finished second overall in the division. I'd hoped to come first, but this was a good start and I was enjoying the job. Christine, Kevin and Justin all seemed settled. We spent a lot of time on the seafront and on summer weekends went to the beach early in the morning before having a late breakfast in a café and returning home around midday before it became too crowded.

Midway through my second year I discovered that one of the newer members of staff had started to steal money. I had an instinct for dishonesty – I seemed almost to be able to smell it. This wasn't the first time I'd had to deal with such an incident – it's almost inevitable with people handling lots of cash. He was encouraged to resign immediately, and, after prompting from me, stated in his letter of resignation that he had 'collected money which I am unable to account for'. Once I had gathered all the relevant records, receipts, cashbook and so on together I rang divisional office to report the matter.

It wasn't long before the divisional manager rang back to upbraid me for not having done my job effectively.

'I resent that remark!' I retorted and slammed the receiver down. This probably wasn't a very good idea, but I was deeply offended at such an unjustified accusation. I had managed to catch someone in the very early stages of pilfering precisely because I had done my job properly. I felt the criticism was totally unjustified.

The next morning my divisional manager was waiting on the doorstep of the office when I arrived. He followed me into my office, with few words being exchanged – I don't think we even shook hands.

'You slammed the phone down on me yesterday', he said, once he had taken a seat.

'Yes', I replied, 'and I'm afraid if you make accusations like that I will do it again!'

A heated discussion followed, which I brought to an end by saying, 'the best way to deal with this matter is to see what I have done first – then you can make up your own mind'.

I produced all the documentation relating to the incident, which confirmed that, because I had done a prompt audit, the loss was so small it was actually covered by the agent's cash deposit. The divisional manager accepted that I had acted responsibly, but didn't apologise for his previous remarks or congratulate me for doing a good job. Nevertheless, his attitude thawed and we were soon chatting amicably about the progress of the branch which was now at the top of the division. Then came the rather curious remark, 'you always seem to know exactly what I am going to bring up or talk about'.

Not missing a beat, 'it's my job to know!' I replied, with a smile of satisfaction on my face.

'Shall we have a spot of lunch?' he said.

Over a meal in a nearby pub, he told me that I'd settled into my role so well that I'd been earmarked for promotion to unit manager (a new name for area sales manager) within the next ten to twelve months. This would see me in charge of about five or six branches and some 60 agents. When I told Christine the news, she was obviously delighted although rather sad that it looked like we would have to move again so soon after arriving in Hastings.

In the autumn of 1977 I was appointed unit manager at Chatham and put in charge of five branches, two section managers, and 56 agents. Within a few months we had bought a three-bedroomed detached house in Vigo Village, Kent for £29,000, having sold our house in Hastings for £21,000. It was in a pleasant woodland setting, with large, open-plan gardens to the back and front and over twenty trees. There was also a good school nearby for Kevin and Justin.

I now had the job I wanted, with excellent earnings and lifestyle. My decision to move from Bridgwater to Hastings seemed to have paid off. However, niggling doubts soon started. I was a senior manager but felt less in control than before. I had more instructions from head office to adhere to and less say in how they were implemented. I seemed to have lost my individuality and was unable to develop my own style and brand of management. This was quite a culture shock to me and suddenly I realised I missed my beloved West Country.

The situation came to a head when I discovered that a senior and well-respected agent, with some twenty-five years service, had serious cash shortages and fictitious policies. This needed urgent action and investigation, as the matter had gone undetected for several years, and I requested specialist help from an agency inspector. Although an inspector was sent down, I only had his services for one day a week. I felt I wasn't receiving the appropriate level of support for what I considered a very serious matter and said so, only to be told, on more than one occasion, 'are you looking for trouble – you have only been in the post for a short while?' I couldn't believe a matter so serious could be treated so lightly and was forced to do much of the in-depth investigation myself, with the result that the agent was suspended and subsequently dismissed.

The company was being reorganised and it seemed clear there would be massive changes and widespread redundancies. As many management posts would go, I began to think about a move back to Somerset. I had no real idea what I would do, but I'd always wanted to run my own business.

I was staying with Christine's parents in Frome during the school summer holidays in 1978 when my father-in-law announced, 'I am going to retire and sell the shop – are you interested?'

'I am thinking about a change of jobs – I could be. Let Christine and me think about it for a day or so.'

A couple of days later we returned to Kent. Christine and I had discussed taking over the shoe shop and we both thought it a good idea, especially as we would be able to spend much more time together as a family. We agreed to sleep on it and make a decision the following day.

Next morning we woke and looked at each other and simultaneously said, 'yes!' We then rang her parents and told them we would take over the business.

I resigned my position, sold our house in Kent and moved to the flat over the shop in Frome.

CHAPTER ELEVEN

Back Home

We completed the purchase of the footwear business in Frome from Christine's parents on 2 January 1979. The shop was double-fronted with two curved front windows and a central entrance. The premises cost us £14,000; the stock, some already marked down for the January sales, came at the very favourable price of £9,000. We had sufficient capital from the sale of our home in Kent to buy the premises and most of the stock outright and negotiated a small working overdraft of £5,000 with our bank.

The business was in Badcox, a secondary but thriving shopping area a short distance from the town centre. The other businesses there included a baker's, a chemist's, a butcher's, a newsagent's, a greengrocer's, a hardware store, a toy shop and the Ship Inn. There was short-stay parking outside the shop, which was convenient for passing trade.

Frome dates back to around 685 when St Aldhelm, Abbot of Malmesbury and Bishop of Sherborne, established a mission settlement west of Selwood Forest on the banks of the River Frome. A church dedicated to St John the Baptist was built, which lasted until the twelfth century, and probably stood on the same site as the present St John's. A market is known to have existed before the Domesday Book of 1086. Frome was also a royal manor and was handed over during Henry II's reign (1154-89) to a succession of families including the Fitzbernards, Braunches and Leversedges. During the middle ages trade and industry became more important than agriculture and the town prospered from the cloth industry.

During the Monmouth Rebellion of 1685, the Duke of Monmouth stayed in the town after a skirmish at nearby Norton St

The shoe shop in Badcox

Philip. There are many historical and listed buildings in Frome and much of the town still has its medieval street pattern. Of particular interest is Cheap Street, just off the Market Place, with a stream or leat running down the centre. The population remained more or less static at between ten and twelve thousand until the early 1970s, but has since grown to more than 25,000.

The shoe shop was established by a Mr Wheeler, who also made boots on the premises, in 1836. He is said to have supplied riding boots to the Prince of Wales – later King Edward VII – while he was staying at Longleat with Lord Bath. There is even a story that he had to deliver them to Buckingham Palace and was concerned he might not get paid – although he did! Christine's mum and dad bought the shop off Mr Wheeler's son, who had taken over the business after his father's death. There was a royal crest, painted on a framed mirror, in the shop. Young Mr Wheeler also had stacks

121

Christine's mum, dad and brother Michael with Kevin and Justin

of historical documents handed down to him by his father, which he promised to hand over when the shop was sold, but for some reason never did.

Although I had helped out in the shop at busy times for many years, I had no real experience of selling footwear, so my father-in-law agreed to stay on and show us the ropes for the first six months. We opened with a sale and our first two weeks of trading were excellent. Many of the old and discontinued lines were cleared ready for the intake of the new season's lines. It was also very profitable, due to the substantial discount we had been given when we bought the stock.

Kevin was now twelve and settled in at Oakfield Middle School, the same one that I'd attended – although, as Frome now had a comprehensive system, it was no longer a secondary modern. Justin was eight and settled into Milk Street First School.

As a family our lifestyle had changed completely. We lived in my home town, I did not have to travel to work and we lived over the shop; Christine and I worked together and I saw a lot more of the boys. We were much more of a family unit and I was under much less pressure. I was enjoying my new career and felt I had much more control over my future.

Fishing with the boys became a major leisure activity. It was something we could do together and enjoy. We even tried to get Christine interested but if she came along she preferred to read a book. Put a fishing rod in her hand and she just fell asleep. The float

Kevin and Justin weighing an early catch

bobbing about in the water seemed to hypnotise her. We joined Frome Angling Club; Kevin and Justin took part in junior fishing activities and I became a committee member.

The Ship Inn was opposite the shop and we became very friendly with the landlord. He allowed us to keep our car in the car park as we had no parking facilities at the shop. The boys were allowed into the pub in the early evening, when it was quiet, to play pool. I was asked to join the pool team. Skittles was another passion of mine – so I set up a team and joined the pub league. My disability made most sporting activities a challenge and prevented me participating at a serious level, but fishing, skittles and pool were within my capabilities and I became quite competitive and proficient at all three.

The business was doing very well. Christine's father gave up working in the shop full time, coming in just on Saturdays, which was our busiest day. As we took more control of the business we decided to change direction in a bid to increase profits and turnover. We adopted a 'we fit shoes' rather than a 'we sell shoes' approach and stocked higher-quality ranges. We introduced a regular measuring service for children to ensure that their shoes still fitted, and gave advice as to when they needed replacing. This advisory service proved very popular. We never pressurised anyone to buy shoes, which gave our customers added confidence in us. Children's shoe sales soon accounted for around 55% of turnover. We also provided a specialist ordering service without making any additional charge; if we did not have it or stock it, we would always try to obtain it. This was worth about an extra £10,000 a year, so was well worth the effort.

Christine and I developed a fantastic working relationship. We had a strong marriage and loved each other as well as being best friends. We really enjoyed being together full time. We worked together extremely well by building on and developing our strengths. I controlled the finances, while Christine looked after the artistic aspects of the business, such as window dressing. She had a particular flair for this and won several Chamber of Commerce awards for window displays. Purchasing and dealing with trade representatives were handled jointly for children's items, Christine had control of girls' and ladies' items, and I had final say on boys' and gents' items and sundries. We both served in the shop and enjoyed dealing with our numerous customers, some of whom became good friends.

As a family we now took different and more varied holidays. During the time we lived in Sussex and Kent most of our holidays were spent in Frome. We obviously wanted to keep in contact with our family – particularly our ageing parents – and friends as much as possible. We now had the best of both worlds – regular contact with family and friends together with the option of going on holiday to different places.

In May 1979 we rented a cottage at St Erth in Cornwall. I had seen an advertisement in a fishing magazine offering accommodation with a fishing lake. The advantage of this was that there was no closed season in Cornwall between March and June, and the

Justin's first carp

boys and I loved our fishing expeditions together. We also hated not being able to fish out of season – we missed it that much! When we booked our first fishing holiday we discovered that John Nott, the Conservative politician, owned the cottage. We had a wonderful first holiday and there was a choice of cottages. The boys and I enjoyed early-morning fishing before breakfast, and there was plenty to catch – the main species being plump and highly-colourful rudd. There was lots to do besides – visiting the numerous beaches nearby, including our favourite, St. Ives, having meals together, playing games and dropping into the local pub. We decided after our first holiday we would be returning on a regular basis.

My early experiences of school had been particularly unfortunate. I don't really blame anyone for the neglect I suffered, as everyone was concentrating on my health and disability. Looking back, though, this seems to have been over-prioritised, with little thought given to what would happen when I grew up. I realised, as a result of my own experiences, that early schooling is the sound foundation for educational progress – I had missed so much early on and I knew now it was a very serious handicap for the future. I was determined I would do everything possible to support Kevin and Justin. On occasions I was probably overzealous and may have appeared hard, and lacking in understanding and compassion; in fact, I was over-reacting to something I had missed and felt really passionate about! Both Christine and I always attended parents' evenings to discuss the boys' progress. We had had one bad experience when a teacher in Hastings had lost patience with

125

Kevin over his 'poor writing and inability to set things out neatly'. Now that both of them had settled into their new schools and were doing well, we made regular contact with their teachers to ensure no further problems developed. Several of their teachers were also customers in the shop and this enabled us to find out how they were doing on a more informal basis. Yes, life was very fulfilling and pleasant back in Frome. It was good for us as a family unit.

In May 1982 we went back to John Nott's cottage for the third year running, the difference this time being that the Falklands War was waging and John Nott was Defence Minister. As we unpacked our bags we heard voices outside and looked out to see two men going round making checks. They were obviously security men or plain clothes policemen, and we overheard them say, 'that's the family from Somerset in there'. Christine and I realised we were much closer to the Falklands War than we'd imagined. We knew John Nott's position in the government, but we had not considered it could affect our holiday. But although this was something of a wake-up call, we felt quite safe with this security presence around us.

We had a chat with the two guys, who turned out to be armed policemen. They put our minds at rest and assured us that we should continue our holiday as usual.

Kevin and Justin thought it was brilliant having armed police-men around and soon struck up a

With Justin and Kevin in the cottage at St Erth

friendship with them. On one occasion they asked if they could see a gun and one of them smiled and gave them a quick peek. They were absolutely thrilled. I am sure they must have told their friends about this special moment many times over.

The fishing lake was small, remote, and largely covered by reeds and weed, with only a few spots where we could fish. On our first visit we would always have some clearing to do before we could start fishing. The fishing was quite hard, but very productive once we could bring the fish 'on the feed'. I would get up about four o'clock each morning to make a cup of tea for the lads and always offered our policemen friends a cup as well before we set off. We returned for breakfast between nine and nine-thirty, and went out for the day at about eleven.

Most mornings we would meet John Nott on the way back from the lake and have a brief chat about the progress of the war. One morning he looked particularly relaxed and I inquired, 'how are things today, John?'

'We have taken Goose Green and there are lots of prisoners', he replied.

'Brilliant, at last we are making some progress'.

We then exchanged a few words about the weather and the fishing, before carrying on back to the cottage for a cooked breakfast.

Most evenings after dinner we popped out to the local pub for a few games of pool with the boys. One evening when we returned to our cottage, we did something rather stupid and stopped the car outside the entrance to the courtyard so that our dog could 'spend a penny'. Suddenly, we were alerted by a sharp, 'who's there?'

Startled, we shouted back, 'it's only us – don't shoot!'

We drove rather sheepishly into the courtyard and apologised to our friendly policemen. I am not sure who was the more relieved – us or them. We assured them we wouldn't do that again. When we returned from our holiday we felt we had been involved in a bit of history and privileged to have met Mr and Mrs Nott.

In 1983 Kevin had been at Frome College for three years and was continuing to do well. He'd achieved good passes in nine O levels and was going on to do A levels. Justin had done well at Oakfield Middle School and, when he started at Frome College in September 1983, was placed in the top group. I was very proud of their progress. They had had a much better start than me and I hoped they would achieve even greater success. I would certainly do everything I could to support them.

Kevin had only been studying A levels for a few months when he came home and told me that one of his maths teachers had told him he couldn't continue in the group as he was 'not up to it'. This came as a complete shock as Kevin had a natural aptitude for maths. I arranged a meeting with the head of maths and Kevin's teacher to discuss the situation. I told them that I wasn't prepared to let Kevin drop maths as this would reduce his chances of getting a place on a degree course. I also intimated that 'if Kevin was not up to it – his tutor may also not be up to it.' I was deeply suspicious of the whole affair and very much of the opinion that the problem was nothing more than a mutual dislike or mistrust between pupil and master. I knew such a situation could easily arise, and had ample experience of it. Why should one man destroy my son's future? I was not having it! We eventually agreed that Kevin would remain in the maths group until he took the intermediate (AO) exam; if he passed he would stay in the group – if he failed he would leave. When we left the meeting Kevin was not sure we had achieved very much. I reassured him and said, 'by the time you have sat the intermediate exam and got your results the whole course will be almost complete and they probably won't even think of chucking you out. The main thing is to stay with it – you will get the results you need if you stick at it – I know you will.' He eventually passed the exam with flying colours – panic over – and another example of how easy it is to be unfairly criticised. I can smell it a mile away – I seem to have a sixth sense for it, probably after years of experiencing such unfairness myself.

On 24 May 1984 I set sail for Ireland from Liverpool with Kevin and Justin. Kevin had been invited to Fishtrek, an all-expenses-paid five-day fishing trip with a group of 15 others, including several well-known angling journalists. It was organised by Paul Harris, angling adviser to the Irish Tourist Board, and jointly sponsored by the Irish Tourist Board and the B & I Line. We would be staying at the Edgeworth Hotel in Edgeworthstown, County Longford. Justin and I had been offered additional places at a substantial discount and we were all looking forward to our first fishing holiday in Ireland. We had read a lot about the fabulous fishing there in the fishing press and had been told about it by many of our fishing friends. Now we had the chance to experience it at first hand, with people who had vast experience of it. It was a once-in-a-lifetime opportunity and we intended to enjoy it.

Kevin had been offered a place on the trip to make up for his disappointment in being unable to compete in the King of Clubs Final in Ireland the previous year. This was a 'fish off' competition for club champions with super cash prizes and prestige for the winners. He had qualified by winning a knock-out competition

Kevin in action on the day he qualified for the King of Clubs Final

for members of Frome Angling Club on the River Frome with a stunning net of roach weighing in at 21lbs 15ozs, but had been unable to attend as he was sitting his O levels. Unbeknown to Kevin, I had written to Paul Harris to explain why he couldn't attend and he'd been offered this brilliant alternative.

We arrived at the hotel and met the rest of the party over dinner. The plans for the next five days were outlined. We would have breakfast at 8am before going fishing to a different venue each day at around 10am, returning to the hotel around 6pm for dinner at 8pm. On the final day there would be a competition.

Our first trip is to a local river whose banks are, we are informed, very treacherous as they contain unstable peaty areas. We take much longer than the rest to get organised, as we have three lots of tackle to unload from the car, and my disability also slows us down, so that by the time we are ready, everyone else has dispersed along the river bank. The boys and I approach the edge of the river with great care. I prod and test the bank with my trusted old heavy-duty walking stick as I cautiously proceed step by step towards the river. Progress is painfully slow and I begin to wonder if I will ever get there when suddenly – whoosh! – it's as though I've stepped into an open manhole and I'm buried up to my armpits. All that's stopped me being swallowed up completely are my arms which have shot out to their full-length instinctively and managed to hit solid ground. My large fishing box, which I'd been carrying on my shoulder, is reassuringly jammed behind my back as well, stopping me sinking any further. At first my sons are shocked but as soon as they realise I'm not injured they burst out laughing. No, it's only my pride that's injured! I lose my temper and shout at them, 'GET ME OUT – it's not funny!'

They come to my rescue, not quite sure how close they can safely approach. Their being several stones lighter than me probably helps. I bark instructions at them. They're still not sure whether to laugh or cry. I think they're stifling their laughter with extreme difficulty, knowing that if they do burst out laughing again I'll become

Fishing in Ireland, a few hours after being buried up to my armpits in peat

even angrier. After a few pulls, shoves and struggles I eventually wriggle free from my unwelcome mucky prison. As I come free they both fall over in fits of laughter. Amazingly I am just covered in peaty deposits and not wet through – although I almost lost my waders in the process. I give a reluctant chuckle and, with my heart in my mouth, continue my wary approach towards the river – at times so apprehensively that I'm reduced to crawling along on my stomach. Eventually I make it and the rest of the day passes uneventfully, with loads of fish caught. The rest of the party, when they hear about my escapade at dinner that night, really pull my leg, but by then I can, with the help of a few drinks, finally see the funny side of it. All's well that ends well!

The next day we go to Loch Gowna, a large lake a few miles from the hotel, with a good stock of bream. We were shown where it was the day before and I am confident I can find it again despite the lack of signposts. We were also told that if we asked in the village anyone would tell us how to get there. The boys and I finish breakfast and rush off to find a good spot on the lake before the rest of the party arrive. You've guessed it – we get lost! Everyone we ask in the village either doesn't know where the lake is or can't understand us. Frustrated and embarrassed, I eventually ring the hotel from a telephone box – one of those ancient ones with a wind-up handle to contact the operator. When she answers, I give her the number of the hotel.

'That will be twenty pence sir', she replies.

'But I've only got ten pence in change', I answer.

'That will be fine sir – putting you through'.

It could only happen in Ireland, I think, as I'm connected to the hotel. I receive instructions on how to get to the lake, only to find, when I come out of the phone box, that a passer-by has already told the boys where it is. When we eventually make it we find we are the last to arrive – so much for my plan of beating the others to it. The lake is crowded, not only with anglers from our party but loads of others as well, and we have to squeeze in where we can. We end up sitting in line, much closer together than we'd have liked. One or two anglers (not members of Fishtrek) start moaning and groaning about kids, disruption and noise. Yes, even anglers can be miserable and unfriendly. They become even more disgruntled when we mix up loads of groundbait and bombard the lake with it in preparation for our belated start. Within about thirty minutes or so we are bagging up. The bream we catch are big – mostly between three and five pounds, but with some weighing up to seven. They come thick and fast and soon we are way ahead of everyone around us. That will teach them to criticise us, I think. Our nets are soon bulging and I smile in disbelief as the previously grumpy anglers wander up casually and ask, 'what's your secret?'

Rather sarcastically I reply, 'prepare properly, and fish where no one else wants to!' Perhaps this is a bit uncalled for, but their earlier comments were unnecessary and unwelcome. We return to the hotel for dinner and a few drinks feeling well satisfied. A potential disaster had been turned into a fabulous success.

On our last day comes the fishing match. It takes place along an overgrown canal we haven't visited before. We do well: Kevin finishes third and I come fourth overall; we both pick up some money, fishing kit and other prizes. We return to the hotel and have dinner followed by a farewell party that goes on until the early hours. Justin, who is thirteen, reluctantly goes to bed around midnight after collecting everyone's autograph, but Kevin, who is seventeen, stays to the end. We all have a great time. I think the rest of the party have enjoyed having the boys along and the opportunity to share their experiences and knowledge with them. Everyone has gained something from the trip.

The following morning we board the ship and return home exhausted but content. Our fishing trip has been superb. Our only concern is that we have been thoroughly spoilt and will never find fishing back home quite the same again. I am very glad, though, that I have shared the experience with my two sons. I know

The Fishtrek party outside the hotel at the end of the holiday

it is something I will never forget and I'm sure they feel the same. We have been in the company of some very accomplished anglers and not been found wanting. Yes, a once-in-a-lifetime experience.

Jan and Dave are good friends of ours. I've known them since 1961 shortly after meeting Christine. Dave always says it was my fault that he started to drink beer – claiming that I bought him his first pint (pints actually!) when he was seventeen, on his first visit to Frome. Christine, who had moved down from Barnsley to Selly Oak at the age of seven, had known Jan since then. Jan had married Dave on 18 March 1967, and since then they had lived in Rednal, Rubery, and Kidderminster. They were now going to move out of Kidderminster and take on a pub at Bewdley. I am surprised Dave didn't blame that on me as well – no beer, no pub? The Hop Pole Inn was at the top of a hill about a mile from Bewdley town centre. It was rather run down but they cleaned it up and trade soon improved. The brewery bought the cottage next door to extend the premises and, as well as refurbishing the pub, added catering and

Dave and Jan share a cup of tea with us in the garden at our favourite little courtyard cafe in Sidmouth

dining areas and a smart new lounge. They were soon doing really well – a reward for all the hard work they'd put into the place.

In the early summer of 1985 Kevin was awaiting his A level results. He hadn't been kicked out of the maths group and had done well in all subjects. When his results arrived he had achieved three good grades and had several options open to him. In the end, he decided to study accountancy and finance at Manchester Polytechnic – a decision no doubt influenced by his keen support for Manchester United! Christine and I were very proud of him.

My mum and dad's Golden Wedding fell on Boxing Day 1985. Brian and Margaret and I wanted to arrange a surprise party for them but had some difficulty finding a venue. Eventually, the George Inn at Nunney, three miles out of town, offered us the use of a private function room from midday to early afternoon. We invited members of the family and told mum and dad we would be taking them out for a pre-lunch drink on Boxing Day, followed by a late

My mum and dad celebrate their golden wedding, Boxing Day 1985

lunch of cold meat, chips and pickles. We didn't have to tell them to dress up as they always dressed smartly if they went out for a drink on holiday lunchtimes. Our only concern was that dad might not be ready; he always took his time and never seemed to finish dressing until we arrived to pick him up – that was just his way.

We arrived at the George just about on time, however, and, once mum and dad were settled in the bar, we told them we needed to move our cars to a better spot. We then drove home and went back to the pub by taxi, so that we wouldn't be drinking and driving. As this took a little while, mum and dad were looking a bit puzzled by the time we got back. They still hadn't twigged anything was up, though, even though many of the guests had now arrived and were waiting in the function room. When they'd all assembled, the manager called us through. The look on our parents' faces was a picture – they couldn't believe all this had been arranged without their knowledge and a few tears of joy followed!

The party went really well and everyone enjoyed the occasion – it was a wonderful party for the whole family. Mum and dad, I know, really appreciated our efforts – once they had overcome their initial shock. Dad was particularly emotional and shed more than a few tears.

Although we flirted briefly with plans to modernise the shoe shop when we took it over, in the end we decided to retain its 'olde worlde' charm, feeling that this made good business sense. Apart from building an extension at the back and demolishing a small outbuilding to create a yard, we ended up making virtually no

Posing with the royal crest

changes. In 1986 the shop celebrated its 150th anniversary and the local paper featured a photograph of us with the royal crest which we had recently restored to its former glory. We also ran a special promotion giving a good discount on selected items purchased during our very special week.

That summer Justin passed nine O levels. He had decided that he wanted to read architecture at university, and asked if he could move from Frome College to Sexey's School in Bruton to study for his A levels. Sexey's had an excellent reputation and, as there was a convenient bus service to Bruton, we agreed. He attended an interview and was offered a place.

On 14 November 1986, I was in the Ship Inn, just across from the shop, with a few friends I usually met up with once a week or so. Tonight, though, was a bit different. My dad was in the Victoria Hospital following a massive stroke. He'd had his first stroke 14 years earlier when he was 62. He'd taken early retirement and enjoyed a reasonable quality of life, but this recent stroke had laid him low. He'd been in hospital for about three weeks but hadn't really responded to treatment, so it came as little surprise when Christine called to tell me he'd taken a turn for the worse. We set off for the hospital, which was only a few minutes walk away, immediately. Mum, Brian and Margaret were already there. We were taken behind the screens to see dad but we were too late – he had already passed away. We spent a short time with dad and had a chat with the nurse, and quietly left the hospital feeling very empty.

On our way home an incident that had occurred shortly after his first stroke came vividly back to me. My father was depressed and struggling to come to terms with his illness. We were having a Sunday lunchtime pint in the Horse & Groom near Longleat, and he was feeling sorry for himself. He said something like 'why did this happen to me? Why did I have to finish work – it's not fair – I don't know what to do now – I wanted to carry on a bit longer.'

I was always able to tell dad what I thought – for some reason he would take more from me than from Brian and Margaret. They always said I was his favourite and could get away with more than they could.

'You ought to be thankful you got to 62 before you had a serious illness', I replied, 'I never had the chance. I had my problems when I was only four'. I was trying to be realistic and continued, 'you must try harder – what would you have said to me if I had acted like you and started to feel sorry for myself?'

He became quite cross and said, 'take me home. I won't listen to any more of this'.

I did as he asked – it was very quiet in the car without a word being spoken. When we arrived back at my parents' home I walked in to see mum. She was surprised to see us back so early and I explained that dad and I had had words. The eventual outcome, however, was that within a few days dad started to come to terms with his problems and became much easier to live with. I'm really glad I was frank with him – I believe it was the turning point and helped him to get on and enjoy life. It may not have been pleasant but it worked and he had 14 reasonable years of retirement.

Although we had extended the shop and built up a good trade, and were continuing to improve the quality of our merchandise, there was little scope for further expansion. We were restricted not only by lack of space but also because we were away from the town centre. It was at this time that a representative from Kay Shoes, who had several times expressed amazement at the high turnover we managed from such small premises, asked us if we would be interested in operating a franchise for his company in the town centre. This appealed to us for several reasons: we could sell the freehold of our shop, thus releasing capital to buy a house in readiness for our retirement; we would be in a much better trading position; and we would have a valuable business asset to sell on when we eventually retired.

A few weeks later, we had a meeting, over an extended lunch, with a manager from the franchise team. He was equally enthusiastic about our potential and told us that we wouldn't need to inject a huge amount of capital into the new business – this had been one of our main concerns. Transferring our current stock to the new shop would be the extent of our capital investment. As people who took on franchises generally had to come up with over £50,000, this sounded like a brilliant offer and we decided to go ahead.

The next step was for Kay's property team to find premises with around 1,000 square feet of retail space in the town centre. We agreed between ourselves to give them a maximum of three years. There was a shortage of large retail units in the town centre and they rarely became available. If a suitable shop was not found within three years, we decided, we would put our current business up for sale, on the basis that footwear businesses took a long time to sell. I wanted to make the move to the new business before I reached 50. If that wasn't possible, I wanted to sell up as I planned to retire somewhere between 55 and 60.

Justin's progress at Sexey's School had proved somewhat disappointing. He seemed to have lost his confidence when sitting exams. We discussed the problem with his tutors on many occasions, but without finding a solution. It was even suggested he try medication, although the idea was not pursued. His course work was excellent – it was this loss of confidence when sitting examinations that was the dilemma. When he took his A levels in the summer of 1988, he did not achieve high enough grades to take the place he had been offered at the University of Wales in Cardiff to read architecture. He was very disappointed and wanted to retake his A levels. I had serious reservations about this and suggested we looked at possible alternatives before making a final decision.

While we were considering what to do, Mendip District Council in Shepton Mallet, about twelve miles away, advertised for two trainee building surveyors. Justin applied and was offered one of the posts. He was still reluctant to give up the idea of going to university, but Christine and I explained that he would be paid to learn, given time off to study and have financial assistance for books and exam fees. He would also gain valuable practical experience. I pointed out that if he obtained good grades and still wanted to become an architect he would be able to change direction, and his surveying experience would come in very useful.

Kevin had successfully completed his degree course in Manchester and we went up to the graduation ceremony. Christine and I were so proud when he walked up onto the stage in his newly-purchased suit – a welcome change from his student attire – to collect his degree. The last three years had had their up and downs. Kevin had had problems with one of his landladies and moved digs several times, but it had all been worth it, and he had made many new friends.

On our way back from Manchester we stopped over with Jan and Dave at their pub in Bewdley. We had done this many times over the previous three years, and we laughed and reminisced about past events. One of the things that had amused us most was the range of spectacular hairstyles Kevin had sported over that time. Dave and I recalled the time we walked into the pub on our way to Manchester and Kevin's hair was piled and lacquered in such a way that it looked like a huge birds nest. Dave just stared in disbelief and said profoundly, 'it just gets worse'.

By March 1989 no progress had been made on finding suitable premises for our new shop. We were rather disappointed, but, as the three years were up, we instructed Cooper & Tanner, a well-established commercial estate agent in the town, to put our business up for sale. Kay's told us that, given the current financial situation, we would never sell our footwear business. We fully understood what they were saying and said that was fine, but told them that, as we needed to plan ahead, we would keep it on the market, fully realising that it could take several years to find a buyer. In the meantime, they could continue to search for a suitable shop, and, if they found one before our shop sold, we would take it on as agreed. It was important to keep our options open.

There was also another serious and unavoidable problem facing us – the new, and in our opinion ill-advised, Uniform Business Rate (UBR) which was shortly to be introduced by the Thatcher government. Having looked into this in considerable detail, we were very concerned. Not only would our overheads increase by around £2,500 a year when the new tax came in, it would, given the restricted profit margins in the footwear trade, be virtually impossible to pass this on to our customers. We would just have to absorb the extra expense. Furthermore, as we were living over the shop, we would still have to pay domestic rates. In effect we were going to be charged double to run the shop, which we thought grossly unfair.

We were convinced, in our own minds, that UBR was an unacceptable tax, especially for small businesses, and decided to try to do something about it. We weren't naïve enough to think we could get the legislation overturned, but felt there would be some mileage in trying to obtain special relief for people like us who lived over the shop. We were convinced the tax would cause many small businesses to close and arranged a meeting with our local Tory Member of Parliament at our home. Unfortunately, this didn't go at all well. He as good as said that I didn't understand the new tax and wasn't being rational, as well as implying that I wasn't very bright. I was furious at his unprofessional attitude and arrogance and asked him to leave. On his way out, I handed him some of the information I had collected on UBR and suggested he read it, adding sarcastically that he might learn something.

Within three days of our business going on the market, we had two prospective buyers ready to pay the asking price. Who said we couldn't sell it? The sale went through smoothly and within three months we had moved out.

I like to be right. It's probably one of my faults – but that I suppose is me and part of what makes me what I am. Why do I mention this? Well, shortly after moving out I was informed that my calculations on UBR were spot on and that the business had an additional £2,500 in overheads to absorb. 'It's nice to be right', I thought smugly to myself. I wonder if my MP had a red face? At least we didn't have to worry about it any more. Quite a relief!

CHAPTER TWELVE

Finance and Politics

In July 1989 we moved from the shop into 1 Goulds Lane, which we bought for £89,000 after taking out a £30,000 mortgage. It was a former police house on a corner plot in the conservation area near Trinity Church, with many nearby buildings dating from the seventeenth century. It had a large and well-stocked garden, with a shed and greenhouse, garage, three bedrooms, bathroom, kitchen, two toilets, lounge/dining room and various outbuildings. There was also room to park at least five cars.

Because the shop sold so quickly, I did not have a full-time job to go to straight away. I had, however, maintained my contacts in the financial service and insurance industries. I was also working about 21 hours a week in the financial services department of an accountancy firm. I had started there about eighteen months before leaving the shop, when it seemed increasingly likely that I would be moving back into the financial world. I felt that, having been out of it for so long, I needed to get back up to speed and bring myself up to date with developments in the intervening period.

Kevin and Justin were still living with us and, as both of them were in full-time work, made a contribution to the housekeeping budget. Christine also had a job for nine hours a week in a local school. I gave up the part-time job in the accountancy firm to take a full-time post with Royal Life as a financial adviser. Although I had my sights set on working as a financial adviser, I wanted to be independent rather than tied to one company, so I regarded this as a stepping stone. Still, it enabled me to bring myself up to date on current legislation and gain the relevant qualifications before applying to work for Kallender Walwyn, an independent firm of insurance brokers based in Frome and Trowbridge. This was much more to my liking and my experience of running the shop was invaluable when advising clients who ran their own businesses.

Kevin, who had been working as a trainee accountant for several months, came home one evening with his chin on the floor, saying he was bored with accountancy. I could sympathise to a certain extent, because – like me – he wanted a bit of buzz in his daily routine. Even so, Christine and I were rather shocked at this sudden outburst. We were both pleased he had chosen accountancy as a profession. It had seemed a natural progression after his degree.

We discussed it at some length and agreed that there is nothing worse than doing a job you don't like. He looked at several options and eventually joined Clerical Medical Assurance in August 1990 as a trainee broker consultant (a representative who calls on independent financial advisers to promote products and provide technical information and solutions). His training didn't get off to a good start. He received little guidance from his manager, being given some manuals to read and left more or less to his own devices. I'd seen this sort of thing happen many times in the insurance industry over the years – new recruits were left to sink or swim on their own – it almost seemed part of the culture. I didn't understand it and I certainly didn't agree with it, but there it was. Personally, I'd always tried to share my knowledge and experience with anyone I managed or worked with. Perhaps it was rather big-headed of me, but I never felt threatened by the people I helped in this way. I'd worked hard to get where I was, but, unlike many of those I worked with over the years, I never felt I had to keep my knowledge to myself in case someone used it to do better than me. We all need help at times, and should be prepared to share our knowledge in full – that way we all prosper. Fortunately I was able to help Kevin with some of the technical aspects of his training. I'm not a natural teacher – I'm too impatient – but at least I was able to make up for the lack of support from his manager and had every confidence he would make it. He also received support from some of his colleagues and, despite his faltering start, was soon doing well and building up some good accounts.

Justin had settled into his trainee surveyor position and was doing well on his day-release course at Bath University. He had passed his ONC in Building Studies with distinction and was now studying for his HNC. He had not only rediscovered the technique of passing exams but gained a new confidence and was enjoying his job.

Local politics now started to play an increasingly important part in my life. Years earlier, before we were married, I had said to Christine, 'one day I am going to be a proper councillor'. Working as I did for the council, I could see what went on at first hand, and was distinctly unimpressed by the quality of most of the councillors. Although some were good, they were very much in the minority. I had been involved in local politics briefly a few years earlier, but – rightly or wrongly – had thought it inadvisable to publicise my political beliefs while running the shoe shop. Now that was no longer a consideration and, with more time on my hands, in 1991 I decided to stand for the council.

My early political thinking was anti-Tory, probably because I came from a poor working-class family. While we may have lacked hard cash we were proud, honest, hard-working, clean, tidy, well mannered and polite. My mother's family worked in the North Somerset coal mines and my father's family all worked on the Great Western Railway, which later became the Western Region of British Railways. This may seem like traditional socialist territory, but, while they were all very determined, none of them were extremists or militants. On the contrary, they were moderate and rational in their thinking and actions. I remember my mother's father saying, 'you never win anything from strikes'. I never forgot that remark and, on reflection, consider it a very profound and accurate statement.

I was anti-Tory from the start, considering it the party that represented the interests of the greedy landowners and businessmen for whom my family had worked for generations. I voted either Labour or Liberal in my first few elections, depending on which party stood most chance of beating the Tory candidate, and continued to do so until the formation of the Social Democratic Party – the SDP – in 1981. This was the first time I felt there was a political party that represented my beliefs. It wasn't perfect but it was a very good fit. I very much admired Shirley Williams, Roy Jenkins and David Owen and became a founder member of the party.

When the SDP and Liberals voted to merge in 1988, I supported the proposal but was concerned that David Owen, whom I greatly admired, did not fully accept the decision and attempted to keep the SDP going. I wavered for a short time because of my liking for David, but, because of my belief in democracy, decided that the decision had to be accepted. If we really want democracy, we must always accept the majority decision; if we don't like it we can always fight to change it, but we should never walk away from it or ignore it. You have to be in it to win it! That to me is true democracy. My admiration for David was dented by what I saw as his stubbornness, and I feel that the Liberal Democrats would have been even stronger had he supported the merger of the two parties – but that's something we'll never know.

In May 1991 I was elected to Frome Town Council as a member of the Liberal Democrat group which won 15 of the 20 seats, thus achieving overall control.

In the spring of 1992, Kallender Walwyn decided to close their Frome Office and concentrate their business in Trowbridge. I was to be made redundant but, as I had been there for less than two years, I wasn't entitled to a redundancy payment. I was offered a position as a self-employed consultant on totally unacceptable terms and heard on the grapevine that one of the directors was confident I would accept it because I had little alternative – he obviously didn't know me very well. I had several discussions with the directors about my future and was offered financial backing, from an outside source, to try to purchase the Frome-based part of the business, but the price proved too high and I decided to look elsewhere. I had already registered myself with DBS, a network of independent financial advisers, because I was aware that this was likely to happen and I needed to make provision for the future.

Within five weeks of leaving Kallender Walwyn I had set myself up as an independent financial adviser working from home. My employers gave me an excellent reference, which was a great help in getting me established. I was now running my own business again and in control of my destiny. This had been my intention when I sold the shop and the timing couldn't have been better. We had some income from savings, and with the boys and Christine

A family photo with Justin on the left and Kevin on the right

all contributing to the housekeeping, we would have no difficulty getting by while I built up the business. I had a reasonably in-depth knowledge of the independent financial market. I was also well known in the town and had a number of useful contacts with local solicitors and accountants. What I didn't have were any clients. My financial backers, together with my own contacts, promised to send me some referrals, but this would all take time. So began another challenge, another test of my determination!

Justin's studies went well and he passed his HNC with distinction. Christine and I were delighted. He was offered a place at the University of West of England in Bristol to study for a degree in building studies on a day-release basis. By this time Kevin and Justin had left home and bought a house together in Butts Hill, Frome a few doors from my mother's home.

My financial services business soon started growing and, within two years, I was earning more – by a substantial margin – than I'd ever done before. I converted my garage into an office, and the outbuildings were converted into a dining room, toilet and flat-floor shower. Justin helped to arrange this and to obtain planning and building regulation agreements, as well as supervising the building contractors.

In July 1994, Kevin, who had been with Clerical Medical for about four years, decided he wanted to become an independent financial adviser. He was a very good and experienced broker consultant and wanted to use his experience in other areas. His company seemed to be losing market share and he thought it was time for a career change. He joined my practice and we started working together and pooling our knowledge and experience, which was good not only for our business but also for our customers.

Shortly afterwards, a financial adviser I knew died suddenly and his business was put up for sale. His clients were predominantly in Oxford and Taunton. As Frome was approximately midway between the two, we thought this an ideal opportunity for expansion and decided to acquire the business. We didn't have to pay for it upfront – the arrangement was that we would pay regular agreed amounts from our earnings over the next four years. This provided an established customer base which Kevin could work exclusively with. Although some of the clients left, he retained the majority and soon built up an excellent rapport with them. The new business soon paid for itself and Kevin established himself as a very able financial adviser. I was very proud of him and felt he was very mature at the relatively tender age of 28.

In May 1995 I came up for re-election to the council. I had been Deputy Mayor for a year and, if re-elected, would become Mayor. Although the local Labour Party was on a roll, with the Blair Factor much in evidence, I was confident the Lib Dems – currently with 15 out of 20 seats – would see them off. But the unthinkable happened – Labour, led by Bob Ashford, wrested control by winning 11 seats. I was among the casualties, along with the current Mayor. Of course, I was bitterly disappointed, but that's politics. If you can't stand the heat, as they say, keep out of the kitchen! Unless a by-election came along, it would be four years before I'd have another chance to be Mayor of Frome. I was determined to be back – but for now I would concentrate on my business and plan for the future.

The loss of my seat brought another huge disappointment. We had been working on plans to redevelop the Cheese & Grain – an old market building in the town centre – as a market hall and entertainment centre. Mendip District Council had bought it from a failing local company and it was currently empty and threatened with demolition. Over the last four years the town council had been making plans to revive it. I wanted it to be used for a regular market. I'd been inspired in this after a trip to Barnsley – Christine's birthplace – to meet up with some of her family after her father's death. We visited the daily covered market in the town centre and Christine said, 'we could do with something like this in Frome'. Immediately I replied, 'we could do this in the Cheese & Grain'. Some of my colleagues on the council had visited the Pannier

The Cheese & Grain decorated for a bazaar around 1897

Market in Barnstaple and were also enthused about the prospect of bringing our twice-weekly open market under cover.

We planned to start off by establishing a covered market in the Cheese & Grain and using the income to develop the entertainment side of the operation. This meant that initial investment would be minimal and there would be no need for massive borrowing. I had now lost the chance to take these plans forward, but there was nothing I could do about it – the electorate had spoken.

In late May 1995 I received a telephone call from Old Mill Financial Services in Shepton Mallet, asking if Kevin and I could go along to see them as they had a business proposition to put to us. I discussed it with Kevin, who knew them as a well-established and professional outfit which, during his time at Clerical Medical, had been one of his best sources of new business. We agreed it seemed a perfect opportunity – but we were only speculating. I didn't ask why they wanted to see us – very unusual for me as I normally like to be well prepared – but agreed to go along.

When we arrived, we were met by the directors and shown into the boardroom. We'd discussed the reason for the summons beforehand and decided that they probably wanted to contract some work out to us. It soon became clear, however, that their intentions were far more ambitious – they wanted to offer Kevin a job.

Although I tried not to show it, I was very upset. I didn't want him to go. In my heart of hearts I knew, however, that the terms they were offering were fantastic and far too good to turn down. So I tried to broker the best deal I could. I told them my son was good – probably the best person I'd ever worked with in the business – and in view of my vast experience in the financial services industry he wouldn't come cheap.

'There will need to be a big transfer fee', I told them.

The team of directors looked at me, somewhat baffled at this turn of events. Nevertheless a transfer fee was agreed and a verbal agreement struck – Old Mill Financial Services would buy me out when I decided to retire. When Kevin joined the company on 26 June 1995, I missed working with him but decided that, instead of appointing anyone else to replace him, I would streamline the business.

Justin completed his course at the University of the West of England successfully and Christine and I attended the graduation ceremony in Bristol – for the second time, another proud moment as one of our sons walked out onto the stage to collect his degree. We'd always wanted to give them the best educational start possible and were delighted they had both done so well. In some ways it had become almost an obsession with me. Christine had always supported me, but at times she needed to calm me down when there had been arguments over their schoolwork and they felt I lacked sympathy and understanding. It hadn't always been easy, but I hoped they now considered it all worthwhile. In all my various jobs I'd always had to start at the bottom and fight to get on, struggling to gain qualifications while coping with the challenges of a new career. I knew there had to be an easier way and I hoped that I had made this possible for my two sons. Only time would tell.

Although I was no longer a councillor, I was very much involved with the local Lib Dems and was Chairman of the Frome Branch. A general election was now looming and we had a super candidate in David Heath, a local man who'd become leader of Somerset County Council at the age of 31 – the youngest-ever leader of a county council. He'd also been an optician in Frome. In the last general election he'd reduced the Tory majority from 9,538 to 4,341. Many of us had encouraged him to stand again. I was convinced he could win and promised to do everything I could to make this happen. When I was asked to run his campaign in Frome, I accepted with relish.

My plans for the election suddenly had to be put on hold, however. I had been suffering abdominal pains for several days and couldn't seem to get any relief. I'd visited several doctors but the painkillers prescribed had little effect. I was in agony. I couldn't eat and I couldn't take my medication without food. In the early hours of the morning I started vomiting blood. When the doctor arrived, he called an ambulance and I was rushed to the Royal United Hospital in Bath. An ultrasonic scan found I had a blockage in my colon and on 14 August 1996 I had emergency surgery to remove around three-quarters of my colon. I had had irritable bowel syndrome for some ten to fifteen years but the real reason for my problem was now apparent – I had a mild form of Crohn's Disease. The consultant told me I was a very unusual case – I was

55 and most people who suffer from the disease develop it in their early twenties. He was confident, however, that I would make a full recovery and that the problem was unlikely to recur.

For two or three days after surgery I was quite ill – but I refused to sleep. The nurses kept asking me why I didn't go to sleep.

'You can die in your sleep and I want to live', I replied, 'also I am keeping my eye on you all'.

I wasn't joking. I watched and checked everything they did the whole time. After about three days a nurse was changing one of my drips and I had fallen asleep – I awoke with a start and she said, 'I caught you napping'.

I laughed and replied, 'I think I can trust you all now – I'm on the mend'.

It had taken them that long to find me asleep – but in some ways I think they admired my pluck and saw me as something of a challenge. I expect they had some laughs and discussions about it, but they took it all in good part.

There was a rather unsettling incident a couple of days after my surgery. I had been told I needed some blood, but instead of this two doctors – I assumed they were doctors as they were wearing white coats – arrived at my bedside and told me they wanted to take a larger than normal blood sample for further tests. I told them they couldn't have any as I was already short of blood and needed a transfusion – this was programmed for later the same day. We had an argument but still I didn't budge. They explained that the blood was needed so that it could be treated with some radioactive substance, after which it would be injected back into my bloodstream so that they could trace where I was bleeding internally. I explained to them that this wasn't necessary as a scan had shown I had a blockage in my colon which had now been removed by surgery. What they were talking about was part of the diagnostic process arranged when I was first admitted to hospital. Still they persisted – they just couldn't seem to get their heads round what I was saying. I became ever more adamant – it was my body and I knew I was right! I called out to the staff nurse who was looking after me and insisted she stepped in to stop them going ahead. She took them away and after a lengthy discussion they left the ward – without even an apology. The staff nurse told me I was right and apologised for the mistake. I had been right to stand my ground, she said, but she was very surprised I was so strong so soon after major surgery. I told her I had considerable experience of hospitals and always tried to understand exactly what was happening and to discuss my treatment with the consultant. Many patients, I am sure, would have assumed that, as they were professionals, they must have known what they were doing. I just don't take anything for granted.

When I left hospital after two weeks I had lost around two and a half stone and was down to nine stone. I looked awful. I gave up all my committees and chairmanships to concentrate on getting better quickly. I still had my business to run and that took priority. Fortunately, within six to eight weeks my weight was almost back to normal. I managed to keep my business ticking over during my illness and Kevin did everything he could to help. I had no problems in eating and didn't have to go on a special diet.

Within a few months I had made an almost complete recovery and my consultant told me he only wanted to check up on me once a year. I couldn't take aspirin, which would irritate my bowel, I couldn't eat green apples, I had to steer clear of too much chilli – but that was about it. The only other problem was that I couldn't walk as well as I could before. I had always used my stomach muscles to support my polio-weakened left leg, but after my abdomen was cut through during surgery, it was never as strong again.

Nevertheless, I considered myself very fortunate. In many ways, I felt much better after this temporary setback. I seemed to have a new energy and concentration. Perhaps the rest and the sorting out of my gut problem gave me this new zest for life and for business. I'm not sure, but my business continued to prosper. The few months of inactivity had caused no real problems, and I seemed to have a more positive outlook.

The investment side of the business was doing particularly well. I had always invested in stock market products myself, as well as in individual stocks, and believed in investing for the longer term, with little risk and a good spread of the various components available in each portfolio. I knew that good management of investments was essential to continued success and this led me to use Henderson Investors to manage many of my clients' portfolios. I liked them because they used many different fund managers to construct each investment plan. They were superb at picking good funds with good managers and deciding when to move or change direction. I had built up an excellent working relationship with them, my clients' portfolios performed well and I received a good commission. They regarded me as an important introducer and invited Christine and me to several hospitality events.

In January 1997 they invited us to the Henderson Investors Seniors Pot Black Snooker Tournament. Christine and I were dedicated snooker fans and jumped at the opportunity. The tournament, which was televised, was held at Goodwood House in Sussex. We stayed at Goodwood Park Hotel and Country Club, and had to pay £40 each towards the cost of our accommodation, to comply with the financial service industry's rules on hospitality. The players, who also stayed at Goodwood Park, included John Spencer, Dennis Taylor, Pierre Mans, Joe Johnson, Graham Miles, Terry Griffiths, Eddie Charlton, Cliff Thorburn, Willie Thorne, Rex Williams, Doug Mountjoy and Ray Reardon.

We arrived at the hotel at midday on Friday and, after unpacking and having a light lunch, went to the bar to watch the snooker stars arrive and see how many we could recognise. At eight o'clock came a drinks reception, with introductions all round, and then dinner, with Terry Griffiths as our table guest. Amazingly, given the dour image I'd become accustomed to from his television appearances, he was superb company – relaxed, charming and a great conversationalist. It just shows how wrong we can be in judging people by their television persona, and also demonstrates how the pressure of professional match play snooker can radically alter someone's character.

After breakfast the following day we went by coach to Goodwood House for the first round and, after lunch, the quarter finals. In the late afternoon we returned to the hotel to change into evening dress for a brilliant dinner – and plenty of wine. After dinner, we went back to Goodwood House where the semi-finals got under way at half past nine. Joe Johnson beat Dennis Taylor 112 to 6 and Terry Griffiths beat Graham Miles 111 to 5. In the final – which was the best of three frames – Joe Johnson beat Terry Griffiths 85-32 and 70-17. The presentation and champagne reception that followed lasted until midnight, when we headed back to the hotel bar for a nightcap. Most of the snooker stars stayed for a few drinks, to wind down after the tournament, and Christine had a long chat with her favourite player, Cliff Thorburn. She'd have been quite happy to have talked to him all night, but he was planning on a round of golf in the morning, and disappeared around 4am, soon after which we called it a night as well.

We checked out of the hotel after lunch the next day. It had been a brilliant weekend and one we felt very privileged to have been a part of. We could now look forward to seeing the tournament when it was broadcast a few weeks later.

A General Election was called for 1 May 1997 and I was delighted to be asked to organise door-to-door canvassing in Frome. We managed a very respectable 40% canvass rate and feedback on the doorsteps seemed very promising. One problem we had to contend with was that, although the contest would be between the Tory and Lib Dem candidates, Labour was fielding the Mayor of Frome, who was bound to take some votes away from the Lib Dems.

The atmosphere at the count in Yeovil was absolutely electric. As the ballot papers piled up it was clear that David was neck and neck with the Conservative candidate, but inwardly I had the

David Heath on the campaign trail

feeling we were going to just take it. There was a recount – and when the result was finally announced David Heath was our new Member of Parliament with a majority of 123. I was absolutely over the moon. It was the first time in my life I had a local MP whom I knew and who represented my kind of politics. What is more, I was there to see it. For David it had been a campaign that had started over twelve years earlier, when he was first elected to the County Council. His record had been outstanding and he had now achieved his ultimate goal. It was history in the making and I was really proud to have played a small part in it.

On 6 January 1999, a few months before his 61st birthday, my beloved brother Brian died of mesothelioma. This is a type of lung cancer caused by exposure to asbestos, which had occurred when he was working with steam trains. My brother was two and a half years older than me and had always seemed so much healthier and stronger. I not only looked up to him; all my life, I had envied his height and his normality – something I couldn't really remember ever having. I was devastated at his death.

I had only known since the previous July that he was terminally ill. He was self-employed, working as a welder and fabricator, and I spent a lot of time with him helping him sort out his affairs – and winding up his business. We also worked with a solicitor in Swindon who specialised in asbestos claims for ex-railway workers, gathering as much evidence as possible to support a compensation claim. By the time he died his affairs were in reasonable order and

*Brian in 1956 just before starting
National Service in the Royal Artillery*

it seemed likely that his family would receive a substantial compensation award. I had done what I could – I owed my brother whatever support I could give him. But I would miss him – I had always thought I was the frail and vulnerable one.

During the last few months we spent many hours reminiscing. He reminded me of a chance comment I had made a couple of years earlier, following my surgery for Crohn's Disease. He had visited me in hospital and said something about how many times I'd been in hospital and how many operations I'd had. I just laughed and said, 'it doesn't matter, I'll be OK – just remember it's the squeaking wheel that gets the oil'. Little did I realise how soon that comment would come back to haunt me.

In the May 1999 local government elections I stood in Badcox Ward and won back my seat with a comfortable majority. The Liberal Democrats regained control of the council and at our first meeting I was asked if I wanted to be Mayor. I declined as I was close to retirement and decided instead to be Deputy Mayor for a year. This would also give me time to get back into the swing of things after four years of enforced exile.

One of the first things I discovered on my return to the council was that there were funding problems with the Cheese and Grain. The Labour-controlled council had taken out substantial loans to refurbish it and it was in use not only for markets but also for musical events. It was, however, under-capitalised and losing money. We had to turn it around, but it wouldn't be easy. Changes to the management structure went some way towards solving the problem but a more pressing issue was the roof. It was waterproof but it wasn't soundproof and, as the bands that played there ratcheted up the decibels, so the complaints from nearby residents came flooding in.

We had no option but to install a new roof at a cost of a further £250,000. After months of negotiation and preparation, the hall closed in October 2001 for the work to be carried out. The opportunity was also taken to install a new mezzanine floor with offices and bar facilities. The work took nine months to complete – nine months during which the Cheese & Grain generated no income. Although this was a major setback, since the hall reopened in July 2002 with an exciting line-up of events and new market facilities, it has gone from strength to strength, and is now regarded as one of the top live music venues in the area.

In October 1999, I decided it was time to retire. Old Mill Financial Services, where Kevin had now worked for about four and a half years, kept their promise to buy me out. The agreed terms gave me a guaranteed income for five years based on renewal earnings from existing business. I also received a fixed percentage of new business earnings, to be renewed, or reviewed, every five years. In return I had to undertake to be loyal and not try to sell my clients to any other interested parties. The deal proved beneficial to my customers (who were happy with the new arrangement), to Old Mill, to Kevin – and to me! It has provided me with a good regular income – long may it continue!

CHAPTER THIRTEEN

Mayor of Frome

As my year as Deputy Mayor drew to a close I anxiously waited to discover whether I would be granted the privilege of serving as Mayor of my beloved home town. So far, only one Mayor of Frome had been born in the town; I wanted so much to be the second. Last time it had been snatched from me by the loss of my seat. I had no worries on that score this time, but I still had to be elected by my fellow councillors at the annual meeting of the town council in May. Although it was customary for the Deputy Mayor to be elected unopposed, there was nothing to prevent other candidates coming forward. As the fateful day approached I rehearsed to myself time and again all the things that could possibly go wrong at the eleventh hour. The worst thing was I could do nothing to influence the outcome. All I could do was wait. My desire to do the job was so overwhelming, the thought of having it snatched away a second time was almost unbearable.

I had a very clear idea of what my aims as Mayor would be. I wanted to promote Frome in the most positive way possible. I have no time for bad-news stories or for people talking down the town. I always want to defend it and look at its good points – this would be the keynote of my year in office. As I have said on many occasions, 'is the pot half full or half empty?' I always go for 'half full'. I look at Frome for what it has, not for what it hasn't. I'd had the chance, when I worked away for eight years, of comparing it with towns in other parts of the country, and this had helped to crystallise my feelings. Life in Frome is challenging, rewarding, sometimes worrying, but very pleasant and, as they say, it grows on you. For my part, it just feels so warm, cosy and familiar. My family's connection with the town goes back around 150 years and I feel very lucky to have been born there.

I decided I would support two local charities: the Frome Hospital Appeal and the Memorial Theatre Appeal. These were two really deserving causes and my aim was to raise at least £5,000. I had no specific plans, but felt confident I could achieve that figure. I would just have to think on my feet. I opened two Mayor's Appeal accounts at the local office of the Portman Building Society and asked the manager for a donation to each – which meant that both accounts started off with a balance of £100. I planned to publicise the charities whenever possible and encourage anyone who wanted to support either of them just to drop into the Portman and make a donation.

The Hospital Appeal was organised by the Friends of the Hospital and had a target of over £400,000. The existing hospital was over a century old and plans to build a new one were being finalised. The appeal was not for the new building but for the equipment to go in it. I had a soft spot for the old hospital as it was where my early encounter with polio started. I had been involved in negotiations with the regional hospital management team in my previous term as councillor over hospital provision for Frome. The chairman had assured me that we wouldn't lose our hospital, but pointed out that its retention would probably mean other hospitals in the region having to close. We were delighted that the threat of closure hanging over our hospital had been lifted. Now, five or so years down the line, we were looking forward to getting a brand-new hospital.

The Memorial Theatre Appeal was supported by Frome Operatic Society who had used the Cheese & Grain building in earlier times, but were now based at the Memorial Theatre. It had opened in 1926 and commemorated the men from the town who fell in the Great War. It had never been completely finished and was in desperate need of investment and repair. It had been used

Frome's new hospital nearing completion in the spring of 2008 and, below, the Memorial Theatre. The Hospital Appeal and the Memorial Theatre Appeal were the two main charities I supported during my mayoral year. On the right, shortly after being voted in as Mayor, I hand over cheques to Wendy Marshfield from the Hospital Appeal and Humphrey Barnes from the Theatre Appeal

as a cinema and theatre, but was now threatened with demolition to make way for housing. It had a seating capacity of 550 and, if it went, we would be very unlikely to get anything on the same scale to replace it. It was a popular and successful venue, and a great asset to the town; I wanted to give the appeal and its hard-working members all the support I could.

The evening of 3 May 2000 arrives and I turn up to the council meeting feeling distinctly nervous. Most of the councillors are there – including all of the Lib Dem group. The current Mayor, my friend and political colleague, Councillor Brian Potter, opens the proceedings by asking for nominations for the next Mayor. I am proposed and seconded – there are no other nominations. The proposal is put to the meeting and all those present, including councillors from other parties, raise their hands in favour – there are no votes against. I have been elected 26th Mayor of Frome unanimously. I have achieved my ambition!

I sign the declaration of acceptance of office, photographs are taken and, before taking my seat to chair my first meeting, I hand over two cheques, each for £250, to Wendy Marshfield from the Frome Hospital Appeal and Humphrey Barnes from the Frome Memorial Theatre Appeal. I'd already decided to donate most of my mayoral allowance to charity and this accounts for about half of it. I thank all the councillors for their support and promise to do everything I can to promote Frome and the town council. I advise them that I would like to see meetings conducted in a civilised manner with all speakers going through the chair.

I receive many letters and messages of congratulations, two of which I've included below. The first is from my Auntie Emily, my father's sister and the sole survivor of his immediate family. She was about 90 at the time:

> Dear Philip & Christine,
> Many sincere congratulations on being chosen as first citizen of Frome – and to Christine as Lady Mayoress. I'm absolutely certain you both will use your personalities and 'know how' of putting Frome 'on the map'. Then – as the last member of our Broadway family – I offer you the congratulations of all those – who are alas 'no longer with us'.
>
> As I read your comments that accompanied your photograph in the Standard I thought 'Ah – our Philip is like me PROUD of our family roots'. I'm a thorough bred Whitmarsh – proud to have been born into a working-class family – with parents that strived to keep us on the right road. I've never forgotten my Dad's words of wisdom:- 'Don't TAKE everything in life – but GIVE BACK something to it'. That, Philip is what you have done and are still doing.
>
> I'm so glad our name hit the headlines last week – as well I recall when I was awarded a foundation

scholarship back in 1921 I had to put up with jealous sneers – 'that Whitmarshs don't go to Grammar Schools'. Well it did hurt – but since then – following generations of Whitmarshs have proved their brains and determination have earned them much success in their lives – & now Philip you have crowned it by being chosen as Mayor in the place of your birth. Your Dad would have been so PROUD of you – as I'm sure Mum is.

Andrew & Christina, Alison & Alan join me in wishing you both a very happy and rewarding mayoral year.

Sent with love & many fond memories.

From Auntie Emily

The second is from the former Clerk of Frome Rural District Council, who was there when I started my first job after leaving school:

Dear Philip,

This is just a note to congratulate you upon becoming Mayor of Frome. I'm sure you will enjoy your term of office & find it rewarding.

I like to think that your early entry into the arena of local government with Frome RDC had some indirect bearing on your interest in local affairs!

I wish you every success, & trust you achieve your expectations.

With best wishes, Your sincerely,

Colin (Hughes)

Shortly after my appointment I had a meeting with representatives of the local press. They asked me my plans and I explained that I would not be drawn into bad-news stories – I wanted to talk Frome up. I told them I would always try to play fair with them and give them the full background to any breaking stories – the condition was that we had to agree on what news was to be printed. If I felt they had betrayed my trust they would receive no further co-operation. They promised not to abuse my trust and assured me that they wanted to support me on my crusade to portray the town in a positive light. I felt confident they were genuine and respected my sincerity and determination. It was about time Frome had some strong, well-focused, positive publicity.

This was the first report in the Somerset Standard:

Frome's new Mayor, Councillor Philip Whitmarsh is donating half his annual allowance to charity.

Mr Whitmarsh received his chain of office at the annual meeting of the town council last night and gave £250 each to representatives of the Frome Victoria Hospital Centenary Appeal and the Memorial Theatre Appeal.

Councillor Whitmarsh has also launched a Mayor's appeal fund for the two charities and has opened an account with the Portman Building Society in the Market Place.

He said: 'it will be a convenient way for individuals, clubs, businesses and schools to pay in any money they raise for these two charities. The Portman has donated £100 to each charity to start the accounts and I would like to thank them for this.'

Councillor Whitmarsh had to wait five years for his promotion from Deputy Mayor. He was due to become Mayor in 1995 but lost his seat in the election. He regained his seat on the town council last May.

Councillor Whitmarsh said: 'I want to do the job justice and I have more time now. During the last year I sold my financial services business and am now retired.'

Councillor Whitmarsh is the only member of the town council who was born, bred and educated in Frome.

He said: 'My family has lived in the town for more than 100 years and I know it intimately. I am delighted to have the opportunity to represent Frome, which I call MY TOWN. Frome is definitely improving and has moved off the bottom. It is so important to get people thinking positively and to sweep the negatives behind us. Too many people talk it down but Frome is far better than what many people see.'

Councillor Whitmarsh has pledged his support to the Wonderful Frome campaign and plans to run a fundraising poetry competition on that theme.

Law and order is another of his priorities. He said: 'The Community Committee on the town council is already working with the police. I would like to take that a step further and reinstate a regular monthly meeting with the inspector (Frome's most senior police officer) with the intention of making Frome a better place to live and work', he added.

Councillor Whitmarsh, who is a Mendip District Councillor and former vice chairman of the planning panel, also wants the police to be involved with planning issues. He said: 'We will be taking advice on their views about applications from a crime prevention and safety angle.'

Projects which Councillor Whitmarsh wants to see get off the ground during his year include Saxon Vale shopping centre, the Coalway Lane Industrial Estate and the Palmer Street development.

He said: 'We need to work hard for the Saxon Vale shopping centre and improve the overall range of shops in the town at the same time. In the short term

I believe Lidl, Homebase and Halfords are all positive happenings – they improve the overall balance of retail opportunities in the town. I also support McDonald's going to Wessex Fields. Employees and customers up there need somewhere to eat. It will save them driving to the town centre and clogging up the traffic even more.

'I think the Palmer Street development is brilliant. It is a welcome redevelopment of unused buildings in the town centre and will provide a good range of facilities. We are lucky to have such a good local developer with an interest in the town.

'I would also like to see the early opening of the industrial estate at Coalway Lane. It will encourage new jobs into the area, allow new firms to come in and existing firms to relocate and expand.'

Councillor Whitmarsh's wife, Christine is also looking forward to taking on the role of Mayoress.

The couple have been married for 35 years and have two sons, Kevin and Justin. Kevin lives in Frome and is a director of a financial services company while Justin, who lives in Bath, is a surveyor for Western Challenge.

I was really pleased with this report because it carried a comprehensive story and gave an excellent resumé of my ambitions, thoughts and aspirations. It was an excellent start to the year.

Most previous mayors had had their diary managed by the staff in the town office, but I decided I wanted a hands-on approach. This was in no way a reflection on, or criticism of, the staff or other mayors – it was just that I wanted to be closely involved with all my official engagements. I arranged for all invitations to be passed directly to me. I then accepted – or apologised if I couldn't attend – and returned all correspondence to the office so a diary of my official bookings could be maintained. This meant I spoke to all the organisers personally and established exactly what they wanted from me. It also gave me an opportunity to find out what each organisation or engagement was really about. Once I had booked the date in my diary I would draft a speech, so that I was prepared well in advance. In this way I was able to avoid any last-minute panic and – hopefully – appear relaxed and confident when carrying out official duties. I was interested in what I was doing and wanted to know as much as possible about each event and organisation beforehand. I'd never regarded myself as a particularly good public speaker, and was often very nervous about having to address groups of people. In the past I'd avoided speaking in public whenever possible – now I was fully in the public eye and I wanted to do my best. Quite a challenge!

To give an idea of what my mayoral year was like, I've chosen a few extracts from my diary. This isn't a comprehensive survey – and I hope anyone I've left out won't take offence – but I think it will give a flavour of what that brilliant year was like:

5 May 2000

My first official engagement as Mayor is to attend the opening of the refurbished Royal Oak on Oakfield Road in Frome by the Devizes-based brewer, Wadworth's. It's a relatively light-hearted affair and, as the Royal Oak has been my local for many years, a good way of easing myself into my new role. Also there to perform the honours is the actress Lois Maxwell – Miss Moneypenny in the Bond movies. She lives across the road and also uses the pub regularly. It is a real privilege to be asked to attend and to perform the opening ceremony with one of Frome's top celebrities. Many of the regulars appreciate that we both use the pub. Some tell me they have never known a Mayor personally before; they are also delighted that Lois uses the pub regularly. She gives me a James Bond book, which she signs, adding a personal message of thanks to Christine and myself. It's something I will always treasure. This is the account in the Frome Times:

Frome's new Mayor Cllr Philip Whitmarsh and Lois Maxwell (Miss Moneypenny from the original James Bond 007 movies) officially opened the recently refurbished Wadworth's pub, the Royal Oak, last Friday.

The traditional local pub which dates back to the 1700s has undergone a complete refurbishment with over £85,000 being spent installing new toilets and a bar and general improvements.

Enjoying a drink with Lois Maxwell – Miss Moneypenny – in the Royal Oak

The new Mayor on his first official engagement said, 'this is a safe pub, which is our local. The work has been tastefully done, and retained the pub's pleasant nooks and crannies to sit in, and the beer is very good.'

Lois Maxwell said, 'I had never been a pub person. But I live close by and decided to come in one night. The welcome I received was so warm and genuine it is now my local.'

Proprietor Nick Hayes commented, 'the work has taken three months to do. I would like to thank everyone for coming along on the night. I am from London and find the pace here in the West Country much slower and far more friendly. We are now ready to offer full meals from Tuesdays to Sundays at lunch time and in the evenings.'

Wadworth's sales director, Fred West, and managing chairman, Charles Bartholomew, were there to represent the brewery and were very pleased with the final results of the refurbishment.

'We have brought the pub into the 21st century without losing any of its character', said Fred West.

Charles Bartholomew added: 'You can spend money but the customers must like the finished result, and this seems to be what customers are saying here, I am very pleased.'

Sean McDonnell of the George Hotel, which is also a Wadworth's property, was also present and commented, 'the work done here is a credit to Wadworth's. How nice it would be if all of Frome's pubs could be upgraded like this and raise the general standards in the town.'

9 May 2000

The Memorial Theatre is the home of Frome Amateur Operatic Society and Christine and I are invited officially to the opening night to see their production of Guys and Dolls. The show is absolutely brilliant and so professional for an amateur society. The highlight of the evening is joining the society and cast after the show at their wine and cheese party. Many of the members and cast have been friends and acquaintances of ours for many years. I also meet many of my old school friends and we have a really pleasant evening. It is a joy to attend and to receive so many good wishes and support for my mayoral year.

17 May 2000

Frome's railway station has been refurbished for its 150th anniversary. Designed by Brunel, it is the only one on the old Great Western with an overall timber roof still in use as a station. My father's father moved from Penselwood, near Wincanton, to work there shortly after it opened. The Whitmarsh family is very much a railway family; in addition to my grandfather, my father, two uncles and brother were all railwaymen. I am very proud to be invited to the opening ceremony at the revamped station and conscious that I am representing not only the town and the council but also my family.

Frome is the only mainline station in the Mendip District Council area, and it is important that it stays open. I remember it from my trainspotting days and, although fewer trains call there today, it is vital for the regeneration of the town. I would like to think that services will improve and that a direct service to Paddington – axed in the 1960s – will be restored. It would be good for commuters and really help to put the town on the map.

This is a an extract from the Somerset Standard:

A £390,000 investment to refurbish Frome Railway Station was officially opened this week amid calls for better train links from the town.

The revamp, which was the result of a successful co-operation between various authorities, was welcomed as a huge improvement to the station.

But Frome's Mayor, Cllr Philip Whitmarsh and Cllr Jim Knight led calls for better services from the town.

Cllr Whitmarsh said, 'there is no point in having a nice building without the services to go with it. We need more links with other cities around the country, not just London.'

Frome station in the days of steam. The milk churns and porters are long gone, but the station still looks much the same today.

Frome Town Councillors have won their battle to get the crumbling Brunel buildings revamped. They have not managed to persuade the service operators to provide a mainline service yet.

Director of Railtrack Great Western Andrew McNaughton said, 'We are extremely proud of the works completed at Frome. Railtrack has inherited many listed buildings and takes its duty to maintain them very seriously. I am sure users of Frome will benefit from these station improvements.'

20 May 2000

The Blessing of St. Aldhelm's Spring and Well Dressing. The well is at the bottom of the steps leading up to St John's Church, and the service is conducted annually by the vicar of St John's in remembrance of St Aldhelm, the founder of Frome. Two of the prayers used in the ceremony explain its significance:

Almighty Father, God of the living and the dead, we praise your name for your faithful saints and missionaries of every age; especially we commemorate St John the Baptist, Patron Saint of our Parish Church; St Aldhelm, founder of this town who brought the Gospel to this place; blessed Thomas Ken, Pastor and Bishop, buried in our churchyard; and William James Early Bennett, restorer of this church. We thank you for the inheritance we enjoy. Help us to work wisely for its future in pureness of soul, and to be open to the guidance of your Holy Spirit; through Jesus Christ our Lord. Amen.

God our Father, your gift of water brings life and freshness to this earth; it washes away our sins and brings eternal life. Bless and hallow the water of this spring; renew the living spring of your life within us, and protect us in body and soul that we may be free from sin and serve you in purity of heart; through Jesus Christ our Lord. Amen.

1 June 2000

Launch of the new hospital radio at Frome Victoria Hospital. Warminster Community Radio has decided to extend its service with additional broadcasts to the Victoria Hospital and residential homes for the elderly. The service by WCR broadcasts 24 hours a day with many news bulletins and specialist programmes. For the first time patients will be able to hear records played and receive get-well messages from family and friends. It is a fantastic new facility. I am delighted to officially declare it open and spend an hour or so at the hospital chatting to the patients and staff. In attendance is Barry Mole, the station director, Dr John Moxon, chairman of the Friends of Frome Hospital, and Wendy Marshfield, the hospital community health manager. The first request is for a song by Max

Bygraves for Mary Aven. Amazingly I know Mary very well; she was my personal assistant and secretary for many years when I was running my financial services business.

1 June 2000

Youth Presentation Evening for the Frome Collegians AFC at the Cheese and Grain. The hall is filled with an excited crowd of boys and girls and when I enter many of them come up and talk to me. They're very interested in my chain of office. I joke with one girl that 'you have to be a good footballer' to get a badge like the one I'm wearing, then tell her I'll be wearing the chain as Mayor for one year only, before it's passed to the next Mayor. I ask them if they know who I am. One bright spark says, 'you're the Mayor', another asks me if I live in a castle. It's a brilliant evening, handing out awards for all their achievements. I also find out they need more football pitches and so I contact various bodies to see if they can assist. This is an extract from my letter:

> The Cheese and Grain was a superb venue for the presentation evening for the Frome Collegians AFC. They have booked it again for their use, as it is the first time they have had a hall large enough to accommodate them.
>
> We are so fortunate to have a building of this type and size in the town centre. It is so encouraging to see it being used so regularly by large numbers and for so many varied events.
>
> The Frome Collegians have over 300 boys, girls and young adults with some 17 football teams competing at a high standard. We should all be grateful to all those involved in assisting our children in these sporting activities, and thank them for their total commitment.
>
> In order that they can continue to function, they are desperate for additional football pitches. I have pro-

mised to assist them in every way possible. If anyone can help in finding or providing more pitches – kindly write to me at the Town Council Offices.

24 June 2000

The opening of St John's Church Millennium Exhibition by historian, writer, film maker and television presenter, Michael Wood, in the presence of the Lord Lieutenant of Somerset, Lady Gass, the High Sheriff of Somerset, Mrs Angela Yeoman, OBE, DL, David Heath, CBE, Member of Parliament for Somerton and Frome, and myself. The exhibition includes items connected with the church over the last thousand years, including vestments, a register of baptisms and a facsimile of the Anglo Saxon Chronicle from 955 lent by Michael Wood, which reads, 'Anno 955. In this year died King Edred on St Clement's Mass Day at Frome. He reigned for nine years and a half.'

In the afternoon Christine and I attend the High Sheriff's Garden Party in the lovely grounds of her house at Whatley near Frome. We are also taken on a tour of the house. The gardens are packed with local dignitaries and it is a really pleasant occasion.

In the evening Christine and I attend the Midsummer Millennium Ball in the grounds of Frome College. There are over 500 guests, resplendent in their gowns and dress suits. We know many of them and the evening passes quickly in chatting and socialising – and supping a fair number of beers and glasses of wine. There is dancing till midnight, followed by a raffle and a spectacular firework display. At around one o'clock, a full English champagne breakfast is served and then it is carriages home. A day we'll never forget.

25 June 2000

Charity Auction at the Royal Oak – the first ever Mayor's charity auction, so I'm told. Very well attended for a Sunday evening. A real buzz with everyone in good spirits. The auctioneer is Reg Evans, a

Jan White, Mayor of Glastonbury, joins us at a garden party held by Angela Yeoman, High Sheriff of Somerset

stalwart of Frome Operatic Society. The star item, which generates some furious bidding, is a three-burner gas-fired barbeque donated by the manager of the George Hotel, Sean McDonnell. It is eventually knocked down to me for £200 – I suppose the atmosphere just carried me away! In all, £670 is raised to be shared between my two charities. It was hard work to organise it all and drum up enough items – but more than worth it. Nick and Wendy from the Royal Oak worked really hard to make the evening a success and Reg was an outstanding auctioneer.

29 June – 8 July 2000
The First Frome Festival, organised and directed by fellow town councillor, Martin Bax. I was privileged to be involved in the early days of Martin's plans to establish a festival in Frome, although I

177

don't take any credit for the fantastic show he's managed to put on. I'd discussed it with him, together with one or two fellow councillors, in the pub after council meetings and thought it just the thing to put Frome on the map. I'd also supported the initial fundraising application to the town council and, as Mayor, mentioned it in briefing notes to local newspapers, asking them to give it as much coverage as possible.

11 July 2000
The opening of the new library at Christchurch School, Frome. I attend the school assembly and several children read out extracts from their favourite books. We then discuss books and they explain why they've chosen the books they have. I ask them if they'd like to enter a competition and write about my visit to the school, with the winner receiving a £25 book token – and they jump at the idea. I then cut the tape and declare the library open.

22 July 2000
The official unveiling of a bronze statue of a fireman outside Frome Fire Station. It cost around £7,000, although the identity of the fireman who posed for the sculptor remains a secret. Jock Garland from the county council, along with Angela Yeoman and David Heath, joins me at the ceremony. Firemen from our twin towns are also present as guests of the local brigade. The Station Officer makes a short address and thanks everyone who has helped with fundraising, before taking us on a tour of the station.

22 July 2000
Mayor's Fundraising Fishing Competition. My father took me on my first fishing trip when I was seven. I caught a small roach and a minnow – and was hooked. I've tried just about every kind of fishing over the years but prefer freshwater angling for coarse fish. Over recent years I've been involved with Frome Angling Club, both as Vice-President and member of a winter league team. I

enjoy competitions and have managed to get twelve local anglers to participate in a sponsored fishing competition. Everybody had to get at least £20 in sponsorship and the match takes place on the River Frome in the town centre. This means a lot of people will see it and can make donations if they wish – it will also serve to show what quality fish live in our river. The net result of the day is a fabulous £1,000 for the Mayor's Charity Appeal Fund.

1 August 2000

Ann Maurice hits town to film an episode of House Doctor in the former United Services Club in Gentle Street. Christine and I are invited to attend the final few hours of filming, after which there is to be a party. When we arrive by taxi at 7.30, we are shown into a reception room specially 'doctored' for the programme, and, along with the other guests, plied with copious amounts of punch and nibbles. The filming finishes around 10.30 and we are taken round the building to see how brilliantly it's been spruced up. The most outstanding feature is the old bar and function room, which has been transformed into an amazing ballroom. This is the venue for the 'end of filming party' – and, as we've already been well supplied

with alcohol, it certainly goes with a bang. Christine, who loves the programme, is thrilled to have a chance to chat with Ann Maurice, and we eventually leave, tired but very happy, around midnight.

Ann Maurice and Alistair Appleton, the presenters of House Doctor

23 September 2000

Frome Carnival: we attend the children's procession in the afternoon and in the evening head the main procession in a limousine donated specially for the event. We head off from Manor Road Business Park before winding our way round town and ending up at Frome Football Club. The streets are crowded with well-wishers and excited children – we almost feel like royalty! Whenever the procession comes to a halt we chat with people on the street. One issue that comes up more than once is the possibility of getting a McDonald's in Frome. Some people are surprised I'm in favour – even though I've stated publicly that bringing a well-known name to Frome can only be a good thing. Because some councillors are resisting it, the idea's got around that I'm opposed to it as well. I make it clear that as far as I'm concerned we should encourage as many well-known retailers to Frome as possible.

1 October 2000

Launch of the Frome Lottery. The aim of this is to raise money for good causes in Frome and the surrounding villages. As far as we know we're the first town in the country to come up with this idea. I've been involved with setting it up for several months and have joined the Frome Community Trust as promoter. There are five draws a week for £1. The maximum prize is £10,000 with 35p

Richard Wyatt from HTV at the launch party for the Frome Lottery

in every pound going to the Trust. The launch party, attended by over 200 local people, is at the Cheese & Grain. Richard Wyatt, the television presenter, is there, along with Euro MP, Graham Watson. Jenson Button, Frome's very own Formula I racing star, is unable to attend, but is represented by his mother. A very exciting and worthwhile project, which we hope will raise funds for years to come, and one I'm very pleased to have been asked to promote.

3 October 2000

It's announced that Cuprinol, which has had a factory in Frome since 1958, is to close with the loss of 230 jobs. Coming only days after Cooper Bussman announced the relocation of their fuse-making operation from Frome to China, with the loss of 200 jobs, this is a real body blow to the town. I attend a meeting with David Heath to talk to management, workers and unions about ICI's plans. We offer our support to the workforce and make a strong case for retaining a manufacturing base in Frome. We accept that there are difficulties with the Cuprinol site, but point out that there is no shortage of allocated industrial land in the town. David Heath and I get together with the District Council, the Regional Development Agency and the Town Council to develop a co-ordinated response and formulate a strategy for safeguarding jobs and encouraging regeneration in Frome.

15 October 2000

The Two Mayors' Charity Concert. Brian Potter, the previous Mayor, and I decide to jointly sponsor a charity concert for the Hospital Appeal at the Cheese & Grain, featuring the local Terry Hill Big Band and the Frome Town Youth Band. A fantastic evening with £515 raised.

20 October 2000

Dedication of the Memorial Garden Plaques. A new memorial garden has been created to replace the original memorial in Victoria

Park and the plaques with the names of those who died in two world wars have been moved to the foyer of the Memorial Theatre. There have been calls for the plaques to be relocated there for years and, now that the hall is being revamped, the local branch of the British Legion has, after much hard work and fundraising, managed to engineer the move. The service, which runs from 7pm to 8.30pm, is very well attended.

28 October 2000

As part of the Frome Millennium celebrations Christine and I attend a Gala Dinner, Dance and Presentations at the Cheese & Grain.

6 – 11 November 2000

The 25th anniversary of the twinning of Frome & Chateau Gontier. I am proud to be representing Frome on such an historic occasion. There are several functions to attend and, to avoid the worry of

Mike and Gill Siblock with Christine shortly after our arrival in France

having to find parking places near the various venues and enable me to devote all my attention to my official duties, I arrange for my friends Mike and Gill Siblock to chauffeur Christine and me on the trip.

We stay at a small hotel as guests of Jean Arthuis, the Mayor of Chateau Gontier, together with Ulrich Burr, the Mayor of Murrhardt (our German Twin Town) and his wife. I haven't met

Ulrich before but we hit it off almost straight away. Taking me aside shortly after being introduced, 'there is only one problem with the French', he confides to me. I am somewhat taken aback, especially after all the hospitality that's been laid on for us, but then he continues, 'they only drink when they eat. I could really enjoy a beer or two right now – what do you think?'

'There is nothing like a beer or two before dinner', I reply, 'as we say in English, I could sink a pint!'

We order a few beers and joke and chat for a while before our wives join us for pre-dinner drinks. This really helps the 'getting to know you' process.

The difference between English mayors and their French and German counterparts is very striking. German and French mayors hold office for many years, control substantial budgets and are powerful decision makers. English mayors, on the other hand, usually hold office only for a year (although earlier mayors of Frome held office for three years). They act solely as the chair of the council, representing the town and council at official functions, and have a yearly allowance of around £1,000.

Whenever we all meet together we speak English. I discover that the French and German mayors chat to each other in English as well. This makes conversation and communication very easy for me. They often ask me how to say or describe something correctly in English. We have many humorous moments and a regular joke is for them to point to me and say, 'big chain – no money', and then, pointing to themselves, 'no chain – lots of money'. They seem to find this particularly amusing.

The official engagements include a Remembrance Service on Sunday morning. Representatives of the German military are attending for the first time. It is an historic moment and a massive step forward in healing relations between the two countries. Despite fears there will be some sort of demonstration, everything goes smoothly. After the ceremony I unveil a sculpture of St Aldhelm, mounted on a stone plinth and created by Frome Artist Jez Pearson, in the Square de Frome, before going to the town hall and signing two copies of the 25th Anniversary Charter with the Mayor of Chateau Gontier. One remains in Chateau Gontier; I take the other back with me to Frome.

From Chateau Gontier's local newspaper

I then make probably the most important speech I have ever been called upon – or will ever be called upon – to make:

> May I thank you, Monsieur Arthuis, as Mayor of Chateau Gontier, and the members of your town council for inviting us here today to commemorate this 25th anniversary of the twinning of our two towns. It is for me, indeed, an honour to lead the Frome contingent on this memorable occasion, especially as there are among us Peter Bargett, who was then Mayor of Frome, and Hilary Daniel, both of whom came from Frome in June 1975 for the ceremony of signing the original Twinning Charter. Peter Bargett will read you the editorial comments from the Somerset Standard of that time.
>
> As a Frome man I naturally have a deep feeling for the town of my birth, and I have been agreeably surprised by my experiences of the last few days – but not including the ferry crossing! The warmth of your

Mayor of Frome

Signing the 25th anniversary charter

With Jean Arthuis and Ulrich Burr after the unveiling

welcome, both officially and from ordinary people in the town, has overwhelmed me. I am impressed by the similarities between our two towns – similar size and population, similar in having roots in agriculture with your own local market, much as we have in Frome; but also like us in that you have much business and commerce to help maintain the economic well-being of your residents.

A number of our party have been to visit your town previously and they are always telling me that I should come and see for myself how you do municipal things over here. Well now I am here, and I must say that as an active participant in local political administration in Frome, I envy the powers and financial strength that your council has to serve the residents without undue interference. I also know that just about everyone in both Chateau Gontier and Murrhardt cannot understand why our Mayor is only Mayor for a year, whilst both you and Herr Burr have been Mayor for many years. It is simply that we are an island race, cut off from so many good things, and we just do it differently.

As Mayor of Frome, therefore, I am also extremely pleased that Burgermeister Ulrich Burr and the party from Murrhardt are here to witness this ceremony. Again I know, especially from Jock Garland, the tremendous amount of effort that has been expended by Ulrich and his team to promote twinning between the three towns.

Twinning links between the two towns have always been many and varied. I know that Mike Evans has been here this week with a party from Frome College. Mike has been here many times. Also I have letters of fraternal greetings from Critchill School, and Frome Fire Brigade. Two former Mayors, Brian Potter and Jock Garland, would like to read these to you, because they illustrate the strength of the links over a long period. In the case of the Fire Brigade that is almost 25 years.

Can I now thank some of the people who have worked to make this commemoration become a reality? Firstly Monsieur Prioux as President of the Chateau Gontier Twinning Committee, who has maintained contact with us through all the protracted negotiations about the plaque and the stone; but also for his help with the Fabriqué à Frome exhibition here last May which was the catalyst for the plaque which was subsequently made. To you, Monsieur Arthuis and your staff our thanks for the wonderful arrangements for this weekend.

Also I would like to thank our Town Clerk, Mrs Rae, for her part at Frome in organising the plaque, the details of the trip and especially for arranging the lunch yesterday. Likewise to Mrs Fraser as Secretary of the Frome Twinning Association for helping to keep the information flowing by fax and e-mail.

On reflection perhaps Ulrich and I judged the French unfairly – or perhaps they understood us better than we thought. Why? Because whenever we return to the Mayor's home we are always greeted with, 'more champagne?' There is no shortage of drinks with – or without – food.

1 December 2000

Late night shopping extravaganza and switching on of Christmas lights – an annual event when the shops in the town centre stay open to 9pm and the lights on the Christmas tree in the Market Place are switched on by the Mayor, followed by carol singing. It rains for much of the day but clears up by evening and there is a real buzz about the place. The Market Place is crammed with shoppers, onlookers and excited children. After I am introduced by the Town Crier, I lead the countdown from ten to one and flick the switch. Horror of horrors – the lights fail to come on. Rain has got into one of the fuses. I apologise to the disappointed crowd while technicians frantically try to sort out the problem. Fifteen minutes later the lights eventually come on – not much of a delay, to be sure, but long enough to give me a place in history as the Mayor who failed to switch on the Christmas lights – another first, but not one I'd have wished for.

6 December 2000

The 102nd Fat Stock Show in Frome Market with over eighty entries from all over the country. After the auction I present the cups and prizes.

18 – 24 December 2000

Official visits to the Riverside Nursing Home, the Black Swan Arts Centre, Chantry House Hospital, Hooper's Barton, Gorehedge Community Rooms, Greenhill Grange, Phoenix House, Frome Postal Sorting Office, the Blue House, Catherine House and Bennett's Gardens.

25 December 2000

By tradition, the Mayor and Town Crier visit staff and patients in the Victoria Hospital on Christmas Day. I really enjoy meeting the staff and patients, and seeing the new babies with their proud mums and dads in the maternity wing – Frome's next generation! After mince pies, it is a rush back home to host our annual 'open house' drinks party for family and friends.

29 January 2001

Frome Rotary Club Dinner at the Full Moon in Rudge, where I am the after-dinner speaker. I have arranged with the chair of the organising committee that, instead of giving a prepared speech, I will hold a question and answer session. A few days before the dinner I receive a list of 27 questions, 14 of which I manage to deal with in the hour allotted to me. It seems to go down well, and after the dinner I am approached about the possibility of becoming a member of the Rotary Club. More of that later!

15 February 2001
Presentation of a £200 gift to the headmaster of Oakfield Middle School. I had been involved in a school reunion marking the 60th birthdays of many of those in my year at school. We made about

Oakfield School: presenting the cheque and the photographs

£200 profit on the evening and I was asked, as Mayor, to present a cheque to the school together with group photographs from 1952 and 1954, featuring the whole school.

More highlights from my mayoral year:
above, with Anne Nicholson at the Catherine Street Medieval Fayre; below, with
Tony Robinson at the opening of Action on Disability and Development's new
offices at Vallis House

Above, Gateway Club's Day of Fun at Selwood School with Christine, Gerald Franks (Treasurer), Sherrie Eugene of HTV, Les Miller (President) and Angela Yeoman, High Sheriff of Somerset; below, Christine with Frome-based actor James Laurenson at a garden party held by Ted Honderich

30 March – 2 April 2001

Visit to Murrhardt with the Deputy Mayor to witness Jean Arthuis, the Mayor of Chateau Gontier, receiving the honorary citizenship of the town. Murrhardt and Chateau Gontier have been twinned since 1966 and Ulrich Burr, the Mayor of Murrhardt, has decided to mark the 35th anniversary in this way. It is 27 years since such an award has been made, so it's a very special occasion.

Easter 2001: presenting an award to the winner of the Easter Bonnet competition at Belmont Nursing Home - my mother

11 April 2001

As the annual civic awards ceremony has been poorly supported for a number of years, I decide it is time to raise its profile and arrange extensive coverage in the local paper, which helps to bring more people along. The council decide to make two awards – to Gerald Franks, who has raised funds for two local residential homes for the elderly, and to Jacqueline Peverley for services to the Mount Community Association.

28 April 2001

Charity fundraising concert for the Trinity Church Hall refurbishment appeal. I sponsor the event by paying for the hire of the Cheese & Grain from my mayoral allowance. The concert by the Monkton Combe Big Band is a great success, with an audience of over 300 and £2,400 raised.

5 May 2001

My last official engagement as Mayor – the unveiling of a sculpture on the Millennium Green. The sculpture, carved from two 1.25 tonne blocks of Portland stone by Kate Simple, is based on a design by Martha Kenyon, a 15-year-old student.

9 May 2001

My last duty as Mayor is to attend the Annual Town Council Meeting and ask for my replacement to be nominated. As anticipated, my deputy, Russell Milne, is elected unopposed.

My year is over. It has been hectic, challenging, sometimes happy and sometimes sad. I know a lot more about Frome than I did when I started. I have met so many new people. As someone born and bred in Frome, it has been an honour and a privilege to serve as its Mayor in the millennium year – it will be a thousand years before anyone else can claim that distinction! What amazed Christine and me was the huge number of voluntary workers who supported so many people in need. They gave their time so willingly and unselfishly. I attended 125 official engagements over the year, as well as town and district council meetings. My charity appeal raised over £6,500 – well ahead of my target of £5,000. It really was a fantastic year and one that I will treasure for the rest of my life. Words don't really do it justice.

I believe it has been a positive year. I have tried to dispel negativity, encourage enthusiasm and inspire by my leadership and example. I feel very passionate about my home town and want to see still more local residents get involved in improving it. I also want to see more indigenous Fromeites standing for the council. Their input is vital because they really understand the town and what makes it tick. I feel rather sad that I have yet to serve on the council with another councillor born and bred in Frome. Perhaps one day soon?

I have received many messages of goodwill from family, friends and fellow councillors, which I find very satisfying as it shows my efforts have been appreciated. I didn't do it for the glory – I did it because I wanted to do it. This is one of the letters I received. It's from a local headmaster, Terry Burton, and I was particularly pleased to receive it because of his assurances that I'd gone at least some of the way towards achieving my goals:

> Dear Phil and Christine,
> First of all a Happy New Year. I hope you had a good Christmas and it wasn't too busy for you both. I wanted to put finger to keyboard to say how we were both sorry that we couldn't make it on Christmas Day. We also wanted to say what a fantastic job you have both done representing Frome. Vicky and I were just saying to each other if a medal could be awarded for dedication then it should go to you both. You have really represented the town in such a good light and you deserve all the praise there is. I think every time I open the paper you are both there. It must take some dedication to keep smiling all the time. I bet you both know how the Queen feels now, with all her public duties! Seriously, well done and congratulations on such a successful year. Here's to you both and best wishes for the New Year – health and happiness.
> Kind regards, Terry and Vicky.

It was a hectic year away from the limelight of civic affairs as well – both my sons got married: Kevin married Karen on 2 September

2000 in Shepton Mallet and Justin married Catherine in Bath on 12 May 2001. Both weddings were brilliant occasions and we really felt the proud parents. This put the icing on the cake of a very special year as well as giving us the prospect of grandchildren sometime in the future.

Kevin and Karen
on their wedding day: 2 September 2000

Justin and Catherine
on their wedding day: 12 May 2001

The final words on my mayoral year go to the winners of the poetry competition I organised. The theme was 'Frome is a Wonderful Place' and the number of entries was ample proof that I wasn't alone in my love for the town. It was supported by the Frome Times, the Wonderful Frome Committee, Premier Print and the Hunting Raven Bookshop. All entrants made a donation of at least 50p to my charity appeal – most donations were considerably higher, but I wanted to encourage as many children as possible to enter, so went for a low minimum figure. These were the winning entries:

Children under 12: Laura Murray, age 11:

Frome was founded by St Aldhelm, many years ago,
The year was 1300 as far as we know.
The town was famous for its cloth and woollen mills,
There's a lovely church called St. John's halfway up a
    hill.
There's a special street called Cheap Street where a
    stream of water flows,
And a market every Wednesday where everybody goes.
The streets are paved with history, we walk them every
    day,
There's tunnels underneath the ground so I've heard
    people say.
The Boyle Cross stands proudly, in the market square,
Up Catherine Hill and Gentle Street, cobble stones lay
    there.
FROME'S changed a bit with years gone by, but the
    River Frome it claims.
It's a quaint and old historic town, and its character
    remains.

Children over 12: Fay Harris, age 12:

Frome is a wonderful town,
It never gets me down,
With lots of things to see and be done,
A Saturday morning is always fun!
Like going to the leisure centre and more,
Going shopping is never a bore!
Or I can go to the park,
Tennis, football what a lark.
And now that Christmas shopping is around the bend,
Christmas shopping with a friend,
In Woolies, Boots and Ellenbray too,

I can find the perfect gift to give to you.
The Christmas lights strung wall to wall,
The tree stands proud and tall,
In the centre for all on show,
Carol singers waiting for snow.
Frome is a wonderful town,
It never gets me down,
With lots to see and be done,
A Saturday morning is always fun!
In Frome that wonderful town.

Adult: residents and staff of Greenhill Grange Residential Home:

OUR town of Frome is a wonderful place,
Where we like to wander at our own pace,
Of times many changes have we seen,
But we still have our hills and stream.
We like our markets, and our cheese show,
Our carnival parade for all to see
Our parks, that fill with children's laughter,
Thank you Lord, Frome is a wonderful place to be.

Friendly smiles bring warmth to us all,
Good friends and neighbours at every door,
Contented, as we all must be,
With many a cheerful cup of tea.
We are unique, with our cobbled streets,
Our winding hills, and valleys deep,
The future times we hope will spare
Our Town of Frome to share.

The Market Cross stands firm in the centre,
Listening to the stream that quietly flows,
Its gentle murmur, brings peace and pleasure
To our old fashioned Town – which – we all – treasure.

CHAPTER FOURTEEN

Nothing Left to Prove

Life is now back to normal. We have much more leisure time and can concentrate on our own lives, but we miss the limelight. We need to relax and take things a bit easier for a while, however, and reflect on our mayoral year together. For the first time we begin to realise how much time we have given up over the last year, but it was certainly worth it – a wonderful experience. A few much-needed breaks and holidays are now possible – it is surprising how much time we now seem to have.

Christine has always loved the garden and spends much of her spare time in it. She looks after the flowers and cuts the lawns. I find the walking when mowing the lawn just too much for me. I tend the vegetable garden and do some of the heavy work – pruning, landscaping, and looking after the trees and shrubs. I also spend a lot of time caring for my pride and joy – a large koi carp pond. Christine and I both love the garden and, although we divide the work between us, we sometimes disagree over new plants or changes to the layout. We have probably had more disagreements – even, sometimes, heated arguments – over the garden than over anything else!

We have been at Goulds Lane for about 13 years and still love it – we have always felt almost as though we are in a holiday cottage – but it is starting to get a bit much for us. We know we're soon going to have to make the decision to move somewhere smaller, with a more manageable garden, and within walking distance of the shops. A gardener comes in for a few hours each week but we are finding it increasingly difficult to cope. It is 'crunch time' and we have to face facts. Christine is beginning to develop a problem with osteo-arthritis in her right hip; I am not as mobile as I used to be, and find standing still increasingly difficult. Neither of us wants to see our beloved garden deteriorate, so we decide to move as soon as we can find a suitable new home. We both saw our parents struggling to cope with large gardens as they grew older and more infirm, and are determined to move while we still can. There's no way we want to be a burden to our family and friends, staying on in a house we can no longer look after properly.

I have joined the Rotary Club of Frome. Peter Smith invited me to become a member after I completed my year as Mayor, kindly introducing me as 'Mr Frome'. It was Peter who, at one of my question and answer sessions as Mayor, asked me what I knew about Rotary.

'Not a lot!' I replied.

He, along with several other members, was struck by my honesty. The fact that I, as Mayor, was in the dark about Rotary activities highlighted a general lack of awareness in the community, and they felt they wanted me on board.

At a social evening arranged by the Inner Wheel (the ladies' equivalent of Rotary), I chat with Les White, a long-standing Rotarian and a former headmaster of Selwood Middle School. He has been particularly helpful in filling me in on the club's activities and has asked me to give a talk on my career at a future meeting. I am outlining my personal and working life to him, going into graphic detail about the physical and educational challenges I'd faced as a result of my childhood tussle with polio. I feel totally at ease with him and suddenly realise that, for the first time in my life, I am talking frankly to someone about my inner self – my thoughts, difficulties, determination, goals and feelings. Never before have I been so open about my disability. All I've given away in the past have been odd snippets – now I am telling the whole story.

I feel really grateful to Les for encouraging me to let go and share my experiences with him, and, a few months later, when I talk to the Club, I give them, not 'my job', but 'my story' – the first time I have stood up before an audience and told them what makes me tick – and why. It's a daunting experience – I know I've got a moving story to tell, but can I do it justice, can I carry it off? More importantly, will they want to listen? The last thing I want to do is bore people by carrying on about myself.

I needn't have worried. They receive the talk enthusiastically, several members coming up afterwards to congratulate me on its warmth and feeling. Thanks, Les, for your kind understanding, inspiration and reassurance – without it I may never have opened up and shared my innermost and most sensitive thoughts and feelings. I believe this is the moment I truly let go and am healed of my struggle with – and in – society. It is a momentous occasion – another true turning point in my life.

Our hunt for a new home continues. There is an open day at a new development alongside the River Frome in the town centre, on land that was once the home of Singer's, an engineering company that has moved to a new industrial estate. I know quite a bit about the development, having attended briefings and pre-development meetings with the developers and planning officers as a councillor. I'd liked what I'd seen and thought to myself what a nice place it would be to live. Unbeknown to me, Christine has fallen in love with a double-fronted house across the river from the Cheese & Grain. As she's convinced that we wouldn't be able to afford it, she's not said a word to me. When curtains go up at the windows, she assumes it must have been sold, and accepts that we just weren't meant to live there.

The open day is a festive occasion, with a barbeque, trad jazz band and drinks. We take a look around the show houses. Christine is particularly taken by a four-bedroom stone-built double-fronted house overlooking the river, then suddenly realises it's the one she's fallen in love with. She decides we should try to buy it. I agree and we head off to the sales office to ask how much it's going for. The good news is it's within our price range; the bad news is that, as it's a show house, it's not going to be released for some time. A further disappointment, when we put our names down on the waiting list, is to find that someone else is ahead of us.

We make several visits to the sales office over the following weeks, and call into the show house to tell the staff we're visiting our future home and ask them if they're looking after it for us! The thing is it really does feel like home, we can see ourselves living there and believe that if we visualise ourselves moving in then it will happen – we are both positive thinkers! Sure enough, when we turn up at the sales office one day, the area sales manager is there and she tells us with a beaming smile that we're now top of the waiting list and, if we want, can take advantage of the 'early bird' system. We have to pay £100 deposit and, as soon as the house is released for sale, we'll have 24 hours to decide if we still want to go ahead. Needless to say, we sign up.

We contact our estate agent and instruct him to put our house on the market. He is very bullish about how easy our home will be to sell, and, sure enough, within a week we have seven offers – all at the asking price. As we don't want to move out until January 2002 – almost six months away – we choose a buyer who is prepared to wait till then to complete. When January comes, we move into temporary accommodation. Although we've completed the purchase of our new home, the developer wants to continue using it as a show house. This suits us as the rent he pays will cover the cost of our temporary accommodation. It will also give us chance to gradually move in over a few days, rather than all in one go. The added advantage of buying the show house is that all the carpets, curtains, pictures and decorations are in place before we move in. This saves a tremendous amount of hard work and expense. We eventually move in on 1 July 2002 – yes, we've had a long wait but we now have our dream home. It's on the level, a few minutes walk from the town centre, with a small courtyard garden at the back and the river bank at the front.

Around 7am on 17 January 2003, three days after her 93rd birthday, my mother dies in Belmont Nursing Home. She's been there for around eighteen months after a series of falls, a broken femur and mini-strokes, following several weeks of treatment and assessment in Chantry House Hospital. I've been terrified for most of my life about losing my mum – I just couldn't contemplate life without her! Somehow, though, I've been spared the pain because to all intents and purposes she died a couple of years ago. This didn't really sink in at the time, but now I realise the person I've been visiting over the past few months was just the shell of the person I'd once known. She just faded away, with no suffering and very little awareness of what was happening. Her death certificate simply gives the cause of death as 'old age'. My mum was very special to me – she had given me so much love, care and attention through some of the most difficult times in my life – she was always there, a real tower of strength, and I wouldn't have achieved a fraction of what I have done without her.

When the local government elections come round in May 2003 I decide not to stand for re-election. I need a rest – and tell myself I'm doing a Paddy Ashdown, quitting while I'm still ahead. I don't want to hang on until I'm past it. Another reason for taking a break from local politics is that it's starting to affect our social life – we don't seem to be able to go anywhere without someone wanting to talk to us about council affairs – our life doesn't seem to be our own. I'm also getting more and more late and lengthy phone calls and people calling on me at home without an appointment. Christine and I are both starting to resent it. I'm becoming increasingly impatient and frustrated; I seem to have lost the ability to listen and feel myself becoming angry inside. Definitely time to take a break!

The next couple of years are taken up with trips abroad, short holidays, low-key social functions, meals out, improving our home and doing whatever takes our fancy. No meetings, no pressure – just relaxing and spending time together.

On 19 April 2005 we celebrate our Ruby Wedding. Unbeknown to us, Kevin and Justin, together with their wives, Karen and Catherine, arrange a fabulous surprise party at the Mendip Lodge Hotel – where we held our wedding reception 40 years earlier. They tell us we'll be calling at the hotel for an aperitif before going on to some myste-

rious venue for dinner. After collecting our drinks from the bar we are ushered into a darkened room that is suddenly lit up to reveal a gathering of family and friends. We break down in tears and it takes us several minutes to collect ourselves. We had no idea at all this was going to happen – it is a wonderful surprise and a good time is had by all. A tremendous amount of thought has obviously gone into the event and the arrangements are excellent. Partying continues until midnight with 'our record' – Acker Bilk's Stranger on the Shore – played several times, together with many of our other old favourites.

Looking through the local paper one day in the late summer of 2005, I spot an advertisement: 'Do you remember the iron lung?' This intrigues me because I remember seeing an iron lung – an early form of respirator – when I was in hospital being treated for polio. I've never been in one but know exactly what they were for. I send an email off to the address in the advert – more out of curiosity than anything else – and, a few days later, Lisa Lipman, a producer from Testimony Films in Bristol, contacts me. She tells me her company is planning a series of programmes for HTV about childhood in the West Country – one of which will be about polio. We have several conversations over the next few weeks and gradually I tell her my story. A few days after Christmas she rings me to tell me she'd like me to appear in the programme and I set to work digging out old photographs and other material so that I'll be well prepared.

At around the same time I'm having a drink in the George Hotel with Christine one day when my old pal Brian Potter sees me through the window and comes in for a quick chat. He tells me there's going to be a by-election for the town council in Welshmill Ward – where I'm now living – and asks me if I'm interested in standing. I'm surprised but also quite humbled that he feels I still have something to offer. I discuss it with Christine and we agree I should give it another go. When the election comes I win with a resounding majority. I thought I'd finished with local politics but here I am back and ready to do my best for my home town. I seem to have renewed energy; I've missed being a councillor and, although I don't want to be chair of a committee or Mayor again, I hope that my local knowledge will prove useful and that I'll justify the vote of confidence given me by the electorate.

15 May 2006 is a particularly bleak day. I have had to take the decision to have Holly, my delightful whippet bitch, put to sleep. Whippets usually live to around 12 or 13 – she's just four. Over

the last eighteen months she's been treated for kylo-thorax, a chest condition that results in fluid building up in the chest cavity. There is no cure and the fluid cannot continue to be drained off indefinitely as it builds up again even faster. It is possible to have open chest surgery but the risks are huge and survival rates so low that we have decided against it. We are so sad and upset; it is like losing a member of the family. Will we have another whippet? I'm not sure, but Christine is adamant we will. We will see.

I have had whippets as pets since I was about eleven. My sister was afraid of dogs and my parents agreed the best way to get her used to them was to have one of our own. They chose a whippet. My father had whippets when he was a young man and I suspect his love of whippets was similar to mine. Our first whippet bitch was called Gyp and I adored her. At a critical time in my life, she helped me to cope with my disability. I loved sport but was limited in what I could do. With Gyp I could go running, hunting and rambling in the countryside – it was a wonderful substitute for other games at a time when I was becoming stronger and more mobile. I owe my

Gyp playing with my sister and sitting on one of the staddle stones
outside our house on The Butts

parents and Gyp a lot. It still gives me a 'warm glow' to think back to those times. Christine says I am a whippet lover rather than a dog lover. She's probably right!

The day after Holly is put down, I travel down to Hampshire for the filming. I have to be there at 10am, so Christine and I set off just after eight to give us plenty of time. On the way we chat about what's likely to happen. Neither of us has ever appeared on television before and I'm a bit apprehensive. I also feel very emotional – which is unlike me – a delayed reaction to the loss of Holly, perhaps? I ask myself if I've done the right thing agreeing to tell my story on television like this.

Filming takes place at Ranvilles Farm House, a olde-world, half-timbered building set in spacious grounds near Romsey in Hampshire. Lisa Lipman, the producer, and Steve Humphries, the executive director, immediately put me at my ease. We have a cup of tea and chat for about 30 minutes. Steve tells me how they are going to film my slot – I'll be asked a few short questions and after each one they'll let me chat away for as long as I like. We run through my story up to the time I leave school. They want to deal not only with my time in hospital, but also the bullying and lack of education. It is going to be tough and the questions will be searching but I'm up for it.

The engineers and crew set the room up and I'm sat in front of a large open fireplace. My first reaction is how bright the lights are. We have a couple of trial runs and they're satisfied everything's ready. Only my head and shoulders will appear on screen and there's a discussion about what I should wear. They want me in casual clothes, as if I'm in my own home. Christine suggests a blue denim shirt, which the film crew judge to be perfect – 'you've got a good voice, you look good on the set and blue is definitely your colour', they tell me. I'm not convinced I'm that photogenic, but they seem happy and this puts me at my ease.

Filming takes about two and a half hours. I'm prompted by questions and given free rein to talk about my experiences. I just have to let it flow and try to ignore the camera. On the whole, it goes without too many hitches. I break down in tears a few times and they have to retake a few sequences, but they tell me that they want my emotions to show through because 'that makes good television'. The most difficult moment is when I tell them about my move from Victoria Hospital to the Orthopaedic Hospital in Bath – a move my mother wasn't allowed to tell me about and something she hated herself for for the rest of her life. Another tricky moment is talking about the turning point in my life, when my maths teacher, Mr Ward, told me, 'you have a brain – I suggest you use it'. I've told these stories many times before without any problem but now I just find the emotion overwhelming. I don't know why – is it the loss of Holly or is something else happening in my life?

After the filming I'm given £60 to cover expenses and hand over a collection of family photographs for use in the programme. On my way out, I run into Bob Giddings, whose story will also feature in the programme.

In July 2006 I am installed as president of the Rotary Club of Frome. I've only been a Rotarian for five years and am still learning about the organisation, but, taking their motto – 'Service above Self' – as my inspiration, I'm going to give it my best shot. Not surprisingly, given my background, I'm particularly interested in the 'polio plus' programme which they've been running for many years with the aim of eradicating polio throughout the world. It's almost been beaten, but there are still a few countries where it's endemic – largely through neglect and denial. In March 2006, for example, only 16 cases were reported worldwide – what an improvement from 1955 when 6,000 cases were notified in the UK alone.

Just before Christmas, Lisa rings to tell me my polio story will be shown early in the new year. I won't have chance to see it before it's broadcast but will be sent a copy after transmission. She asks for details of local papers so that she can send press releases out.

A few weeks later I am contacted by the Western Daily Press, the Frome Times and the Somerset Standard. I have my photograph taken and give yet more interviews – and find once again that my emotions are severely tested when discussing my most traumatic memories. At times I find it difficult not to a shed a few tears – this is absolutely incredible – I seem to have changed.

One of the reporters who calls to interview me is Caroline Wood from the Somerset Standard. When I was Mayor, she did an article on my childhood with the heading. 'This lad grew up to be Mayor of Frome'. We cover much the same ground, but, whereas six years ago I got through the interview without any particular show of emotion, this time I can hardly keep the tears back. When I tell her I can't understand what's happened, 'I think I know what the answer is', she replies, 'you have nothing to prove anymore'. Maybe she's right.

The programme – called appropriately Reaching for Dreams – goes out at 7.30pm on 6 February 2007. It receives widespread publicity – the Western Daily Press has an article with photographs on the front page and a double-page spread inside; ITV West (the new name for HTV) runs lengthy trailers for it throughout the day.

As soon as it's over, the telephone starts ringing and, for the next hour or so, family, friends, fellow councillors, Rotarians and old school mates tell me how moving they found it – some are absolutely amazed what I had to go through. For several weeks afterwards I continue to receive telephone calls, letters, e-mails and postcards; when I go out, people keep stopping me in the street. Testimony Films contact me to say that, of the six programmes in the series, it had by far the best ratings.

I make contact with Bob Giddings and Bridget Langdon, whose stories also featured in the programme. Bob and I become good friends and he suggests I write my story.

'You have some good stories, you must do it', he tells me, 'get yourself a publisher'.

Another friend of mine, Professor Ted Honderich, who used to be my neighbour in Goulds Lane, missed the television programme and comes round to watch the recording – and sheds a few tears during it. I tell him what Bob has said.

'Can you do it? he asks.

'I don't know', I reply, 'I've sketched out some early chapters. Take them away and tell me what you honestly think. I don't want to waste my time if the story is no good.'

A few days later he returns my manuscript with a note: 'Nothing should stop you finishing your book. It is lovely. So human, engrossing, honest, suspenseful and fluent. I think you will probably get a publisher, but even if that doesn't happen you must finish the thing. It seems to me certain that it is an entirely valuable project for you to do, and it is important to have a record of your singular life, important for more than your family.'

With Ted Honderich in the garden of his home

I've said to Christine many times over the years that I want to tell my life story. She told me I should just start writing. Other people have said much the same thing – but I knew inwardly that the time had to be right. I wasn't sure I could do it – I'm still not – but all I can do is tell it like it is.

One person I'd like to pay particular tribute to is John Moxon, a fellow senior Rotarian and retired GP. He was the editor of the Frome Rotary Club Newsletter, so I shared lots of my thoughts with him. Like me he is a strong character – sometimes we clashed – but not any longer – we now seem to fully understand each other and are firm friends. It's amazing how history seems to repeat itself – many of my friendships have grown from similar battles with strong characters over the years – what does that say about me? He has given me encouragement all the way along and was one of the first people to ring me after the television programme. He later wrote something in the Rotary newsletter that touched me almost more than anything else: 'Phil shone like a star and won everyone's admiration for his determination to fight his disability as a small child and catch up on his education where no provision was made and unkind prejudice from his peers had to be surmounted. This has allowed him to lead a full and active life. What a success he has made and we can understand why he champions so strongly those he feels unfairly criticised.' Thanks John!

Encouragement from Bob, Ted, Les and Christine was a vital factor in getting me to start setting my story down. I hope they were right – because this is it! My story in a nutshell is 'this little crippled boy grew up to be Mayor of Frome'. I often describe my life, particularly the early part of it, as 'my rough and tumble with polio' or 'my tussle with polio'. I see it as a fight or struggle because that is how it was – I wouldn't let people push me around – the more they pushed the more I resisted – hence the title of this book – 'I'm Not Prepared to Accept That!' It's something I often say when I'm in difficult or heavy negotiations – it always stops the conversation stone dead – I believe it is so powerful because the message comes loud and clear from my inner soul – I suppose it is my knock-out punch. As my friends and associates say, 'there's no answer to that!'

The bullies tried and tried and I just took them all on – in some ways I was never afraid of the outcome, because I couldn't run away – it was a physical impossibility. I had to stand up and face the music no matter how big or strong my opponent was. I was so small and weak in those days that all the odds were stacked against me, but I only ever had one real hiding in my life. I knew that the first punch was the only one you felt, so I made sure that mine was the first and that it was hard and aimed straight at the nose. Most fights ended with that. Perhaps I was lucky, or protected in some way, or just plain determined, but all bullying stopped by the time I was ten. I'd already realised by then that I couldn't continue in this way because in the end all fighters lose – 'someone will always come along and defeat the champion' to quote a boxing term. So the penny dropped and I accepted that my tongue had to become my sword. I can't say it happened overnight, but I haven't had a fight since leaving school, and only a couple after I was eleven. Perhaps I'm a quicker learner than I give myself credit for!

What does it all now mean? What do I think when I look back over my life? I know one thing for certain – as I have told my story I can't believe I did some of it – it seems almost like a dream – where did I find the strength or courage to take on these challenges? I suppose I acted the way I did because I had no alternative – I could not run away – I never would anyway – I believe you must face up to reality straight away – it is no use putting it off because it will not go away. It will just get worse. I also know I was never afraid of the consequences of my actions – yes, I may have been nervous but that never ever stopped me. I was so determined not to accept anything that I felt was wrong or unfair – equally I would also stand up for others. I may not always be right but I have always wanted justice and fairness. I think some of this resolve came from my mum, with her quiet strength, and my Auntie Emily, with her determination to succeed educationally. It was in my genes.

During my time in the insurance industry I hated targets or goals. I always felt they never really achieved what they were meant to. Why? Because they were either unachievable or too easy – either way they failed. If a target is too high you don't try to reach it because you know you can't – it just demotivates you; successful producers are often ruined by being given unrealistic goals. If it is too soft the temptation is to switch off when you reach it. But this may also explain something about me. I have always had personal targets and having set them I want to achieve them. I also believe it is important to have a balance in life. Not too much work or too much play. Perhaps my motivation was my own individual quest for achievement. Was this what drove me on? I am convinced that if you believe something will happen – and believe it honestly and strongly enough – then it will happen. A few months ago, for example, I attended a seminar and there was a laptop computer as a prize. I wanted it – I focused on it as soon as I was invited to the course – I visualised it becoming mine when it was put on display – and I won it!

This is how some of my goals turned out:

1) To be treated like a normal person: I could not change my disability but I could change the way I was treated by others. I wanted to work, to have a proper job and financial security and not be a passenger. A friend recently wrote to me saying, 'you are no different to anyone else'. Other people tell me, 'we never notice your limp'. I am, in their eyes, a normal person.

2) To be happily married: I married Christine in 1965 over 42 years ago. We have had our difficulties and that is normal, but you have to resolve them by discussing them and working them through. We are best of friends and have always been honest and open with each other. We still enjoy being together.

3) To have children and grandchildren: We have our two sons Kevin and Justin; they are now married with successful careers. We also have three wonderful grandchildren – Kevin and Karen have Millie

(born 4 August 2001) and Samuel (born 10 September 2005); Justin and Catherine have Daisy (born 20 February 2006). We hope for many more pleasurable years watching the next generation of our family grow up.

4) To run my own business: Working in the insurance industry was almost like running my own business. From there I went on to run the shoe shop for ten years before working as an independent financial adviser, running my own organisation, until I retired.

5) To own a winning racehorse: I have always loved horseracing, but hate losing money so I'm not a habitual gambler – the name Philip means 'lover of horses' so I run true to form! I have been involved with a syndicate called Nineways for several years and have been in the winner's enclosure twice as well as having several placings. We have another horse – Master Belle – with trainer Ron Hodges and remain hopeful for the future.

In the winners' enclosure at Exeter on 23 March 2004 with Kevin Corcoran, Tony McCoy and Noble Calling and Martyn Peters, another member of the Nineways syndicate

6) To be a proper councillor: Yes, I even became Mayor, and I hope that can be classed as another success.

7) To write a book: Almost there!

Hospital treatment has changed enormously since 1945. Back then, there was an iron discipline and shutting children away was considered the correct thing to do. Visiting was not encouraged. My poor mum was told not to tell me I was being moved from one hospital to another – she so much loathed that moment – in those days doctors and nurses were never questioned – she just had to accept it. No one told you anything. It was all so mysterious. The situation is very different now – the change in attitudes towards children and their rights is incredible. At least they don't have to remain in fear of the unknown – although to be fair I'm not sure it affected me too much, except perhaps for making me over sensitive and too quick to react to anything I see as criticism.

Now our new hospital is being built after ten years of campaigning. It is an especial delight for me to have been involved in a modest way in helping to bring this about. As a district councillor I served on the planning committee that approved the planning application, and during my term as Mayor the hospital appeal was one of my chosen charities. It was a wonderful experience to be able to support the Friends of the Hospital in their fundraising activities. They have now accumulated over half a million pounds to purchase equipment for the new hospital. I would like, on behalf of the town, to really thank them for their hard work over many years to raise this money and bravely and tirelessly to fight for our new hospital. It is a fantastic achievement when so many hospitals are closing, particularly over the border in Wiltshire. I hope to continue my support for the new hospital when it opens in spring 2008 – I already have some ideas.

My year as president of the Frome Rotary Club comes to an end on 9 July 2007, and I hand over the mantle to Ray Barnes – I've

Above, Rotary Club President's Night, 25 May 2007, with top table guests; below, handing over the presidency to Ray Barnes

known him for around 40 years and am sure he will bring new ideas and enthusiasm to the club. My year has had its ups and downs. I have presided over some major changes – our meetings now take place at Frome Rugby Club and they

215

are no longer all held at lunchtimes – a programme of breakfast, lunchtime, evening and twilight meetings has been drawn up to make it easier for busy members to attend more often. I have championed and resisted criticism of members in public, and always sought to encourage them. I believe the club is much more relaxed and happier now. My year hasn't always been enjoyable but I think the club is in good shape to move forward.

If possible, I want to use my book, when it's published, to promote the total eradication of polio – I can see another challenge coming up! I wonder how many Rotary presidents have suffered with polio? One thing I do know is that there is no longer any need for anyone to suffer with it today. Another push could see it eliminated worldwide. I already have some ideas!

At the local council elections in May 2007 I am elected as a councillor for Mendip District Council and Frome Town Council representing the Market Ward – renamed after boundary changes but still covering the area in which I live. In July 2007 I am appointed shadow portfolio holder for regeneration, something very close to my heart. I am delighted to accept the challenge – and it will be just that as no party has overall control. It is wonderful to be recognised as someone who still has something to offer. Long may it continue! Who says I'm retired?

One thing I have learnt from life is that respect is a very special thing. I believe I have now got that. It is something I deeply treasure – something you can only earn – something you cannot ever demand.

Incidents – even minor incidents – at an early age can sometimes have repercussions right through your life. One of my teachers said to my parents at a parents' evening when I was studying for GCEs, 'Philip has no leadership qualities whatsoever – I am not sure what the future holds for him'. I'm sure he was wrong – but his saying that made me try that bit harder just to prove him wrong!

I still have some unfinished goals for the future. Christine knows what they are. Will they happen? Watch this space!

These are my final thoughts. I don't think I am especially brave, courageous or anything like that – I just kept trying. I was also lucky to have people around me who inspired, encouraged and believed in me. They always seemed to be there when I needed them. To be honest, as I said before, I had no other alternative – that is simply the way I see it and the way it was. It is better to have a go and fail

With Nick Clegg on the campaign trail in 2007 in David Heath's constituency office

than never try at all. What I do know is that people who are disabled fall into two distinct groups – the 'doers' and the 'don'ters'. Always be positive and believe you will come through – truly believe it and you will! Be a 'doer'. Just keep striving! And keep smiling! I hope my story will be an inspiration to others. If you are disabled or disadvantaged in any way – DON'T GIVE UP! I truly hope this book will encourage, influence and help others suffering from any disability or disadvantage to try and try – again and again. I hope and pray it will ignite a flame of determination and create a hotspot of intense and vigorous energy to rise above and overcome any unwanted obstacles. Many children have gone through worse than me and come out on top – so there are no barriers – go for it!

And next time someone or something puts a barrier in your way, remember my lifelong motto and say, 'I'M NOT PREPARED TO ACCEPT THAT!'

APPENDIX ONE

The Orthopaedic Surgeons

Writing my story prompted many memories and made me curious about many aspects of my early life. In particular, I began to wonder about the people who treated me. I was certainly indebted to them – without their skill and expertise I would not have been able to achieve what I have. They gave me an almost normal life, but I knew very little about them. So I decided to find out more.

Medical treatment was very different in 1945. The watchword was secrecy; no one told you anything or explained very much. Hospitals were strict and tightly regulated, visiting, particularly for children, very limited. There was, however, an air of competence and professionalism that encouraged confidence. I never wavered in my belief that 'hospitals were there to make you better'. Much of the work they did was new and untried, but as patients we were never informed about the risks. We did not even know the Christian names of many of our consultants and doctors, let alone their interests, abilities and expertise. I have become intrigued by their history and would like to share some of what I have discovered about them.

I am grateful to Tina Craig, Deputy Head of Library and Information Services at the Royal College of Surgeons of England, 35-43 Lincoln's Inn Fields, London WC2A 3PE; she has been very supportive in my research. If anyone has any more information, I would be delighted to receive it. I can be contacted at: philchris@telecomplus.org.uk.

JOHN BASTOW, MRCS, FRCS, BS (Melbourne), MD (1906-65)
John Bastow diagnosed me with infantile paralysis (now known as poliomyelitis). He was born in India; his father, a civil engineer, was

Australian, and his mother came from Devon. He was educated in Australia and studied medicine at Ormond College, University of Melbourne, graduating in 1927. He then went to Alfred Hospital in Melbourne, where he held house appointments, became a medical registrar and obtained his doctorate in 1931.

Shortly after arriving in England he was appointed house surgeon to the Robert Jones and Agnes Hunt Orthopaedic Hospital at Oswestry in Shropshire. He also met his future wife at Oswestry. Through his connections with Sir Harry Platt and Sir Reginald Watson-Jones he decided to become an orthopaedic surgeon. After studying at St Bartholomew's Hospital, he took his Fellowship in 1932.

He was appointed to the staff of Bath & Wessex Orthopaedic Hospital in 1934 and, in association with Charles Kindersley, developed an excellent orthopaedic service and later became senior orthopaedic surgeon. He encouraged corporate spirit amongst consultants and was considered a wise counsellor and natural leader.

At school he was a keen athlete, and his interest in sport – especially cricket, shooting and fishing – remained with him all his life. In March 1964, as a result of a shooting accident, he received wounds from which he never recovered. He died on 1 January 1965.

MAUD FRANCES FORRESTER-BROWN, MB, ChB, MD (London), MS (1885-1970)

Miss Forrester-Brown determined and controlled most of my treatment. She was a formidable, outspoken and influential character – I often wonder if her strength of character influenced me.

Born in London, she attended Bedford High School after spending her early childhood in India. She studied at London School of Medicine for Women and was a Gilchrist Student at the University of London.

At the Royal Hospital for Sick Children she was house surgeon to Sir Harold Stiles. This association resulted in her joining the staff of the War Hospital at Bangour near Edinburgh where she met Sir Robert Jones, a friend of Sir Harold Stiles, and orthopaedics became her chosen field. Sir Robert Jones was influenced by his uncle, Sir Hugh Owen Thomas, who came from a long line of bone-setters and is regarded as the father of orthopaedics. She went to Oswestry with Sir Robert Jones after a spell in Liverpool studying orthopaedics.

Miss Forrester-Brown was appointed orthopaedic surgeon at the Bath & Wessex Orthopaedic Hospital shortly after it was founded in 1924 and developed a network of specialist clinics throughout Somerset, Wiltshire and Dorset. Illnesses such as TB, rickets and polio were commonplace and there was much apathy, hostility and ignorance to be overcome. She was very much a pioneer, drawing on her experience at Oswestry, but continually developing new ideas. Posture was important to her and she campaigned for the introduction of suitable desks and chairs into schools, as well as a programme of daily exercise for children. She also worked with shoemakers to produce better footwear for children. She was

involved in the installation of a swimming pool at the hospital in Bath as a memorial to Sir Robert Jones. After retiring in 1951 she was appointed Emeritus Consultant to the Bath & Wessex Orthopaedic Hospital.

There is no doubt she loved her work and cared for her patients. Her energy, enthusiasm

Miss Forrester-Brown chatting to some of her patients

and passion were self evident. She liked to check on the progress of her patients at first hand and made regular ward visits. She also had an insatiable appetite for knowledge and travelled worldwide – to America, Italy, Denmark, Sweden and the Philippines – spending her vacations at orthopaedic clinics. The work of Professor Vittorio in Italy was very influential in her development of splints; she also translated some of his articles into English. She was involved with many medical societies and associations, supporting them in a variety of ways. She was a Member of the British Medical Association for more than 50 years and joined the British Orthopaedic Association in 1921.

Her outside interests were considerable: she managed to find time for drama, sculpture, painting, skiing, skating, horse-riding, golf and swimming. She could speak five languages fluently and learnt Spanish when she was over 60. Fitness was an important part of her life and she continued to ride horses and swim until well into her eighties. She is on record as saying on several occasions, after a spell of sickness or an injury, that she would not get better until she got on a horse.

She died on 12 January 1970 in Edinburgh Royal Infirmary.

HEDLEY WALTER HALL, MRCS, FRCS, MB, BS (London), LRCP (1907-2003)

Hedley Hall took over from Miss Forrester-Brown when she retired in 1951. He was a quiet thoughtful man, in complete contrast to his predecessor. Although under his care for only a short time, he performed the operation on my right knee to slow down the growth of my leg.

Born in Farsley near Leeds, he was educated at Goole Primary School, Goole Secondary School and Shebbear College in Devon. He studied medicine at King's College, London and clinical studies at University College Hospital. He was house surgeon at University College Hospital and registrar at the Central Middlesex Hospital before moving to the Royal National Orthopaedic Hospital. Philip Wiles, Norman Matheson and Illtyd James influenced much of his work and training.

From 1947 to 1949 he was a major in the RAMC. He was consultant orthopaedic surgeon to the North Middlesex Hospital before taking up a similar post in Bath. He was also consultant orthopaedic surgeon to the Shaftesbury Home at Malmesbury.

His outside interests included cricket, archaeology, gardening, beekeeping, literature, theatre and travel. He was president of Hinton Charterhouse Cricket Club and played cricket until he was over 50. He was also a governor of Shebbear College.

He died on 22 September 2003.

TOM PRICE, MCh (Orth) (Liverpool) (1914-67)

I really liked this man. I had so much in common with him and he always had a smile for me. I believe we had a special rapport. He had one leg shorter than the other and wore a built-up surgical boot, so in many ways I was like him. He took over from Hedley

Hall and was my final consultant. I remained in his care until I was discharged, and, although he did not operate on me, he supervised the removal of my callipers and encouraged me to walk unaided.

I think he was proud of the successful treatment I received at Bath & Wessex Orthopaedic Hospital and the part he played in it. Just as I was about to leave his clinic, when my treatment was complete, he invited me to attend a seminar where he was discussing some of his poliomyelitis patients. He used me as a good example of what could be physically achieved.

He was born with a congenital dislocation of both hips, which left him with a permanent disability. He qualified in medicine in 1939 and, after serving with the RAMC in India and Pakistan, trained in orthopaedics at Liverpool. In 1948 he was appointed to the staff of Bath & Wessex Orthopaedic Hospital as an orthopaedic surgeon. He had a special interest in the care of children and supported many clinics in Somerset and Wiltshire. He retired in 1964. Although battling for most of his life with disability and malignant hypertension, he was courageous, caring, enthusiastic and inspirational, and never let his personal problems distract him from the job in hand.

He retired to Heswall, Liverpool and continued to attend ward rounds at the Royal Liverpool Children's Hospital.

He died in 1967.

APPENDIX TWO

The Mayor's Chain

The Mayor's Badge of Office, a replica of the coat of arms in enamelled and gilded solid silver made by local jeweller TH Vincent, was presented to Frome Urban District Council on 6th December 1954 by the Chamber of Commerce. It was attached to a gilt chain provided by a local firm, JW Singer & Sons, with subscriptions from members of the council.

Following local government reorganisation in 1974, the Urban District Council was replaced by Mendip District Council. Frome elected to have a Town Council and Mayor. The Mayor as chief citizen now wears the badge and the links are engraved with the names of past Mayors.

By letters patent dated 14 August 1953 the kings at arms granted armorial bearings to Frome Urban District Council. By an endorsement on the reverse of the letters patent, the Queen, in exercise of the powers conferred on her by the Local Government Act 1972, by order in Council dated 21 June 1974, authorised the bearing and use by Frome Town Council of the armorial bearings borne before 1 April 1974 by Frome Urban District Council.

The shield is sable (black), a colour chosen because it is common to the arms of both the Worshipful Company of Clothworkers – a reminder of Frome's connection with the cloth industry – and the Leversedge family, who were Lords of the Manor between the fifteenth and eighteenth centuries.

The shield bears an inverted double chevron, ermine (white with black markings representing stoats' tails) on gold. The ermine chevron and the gold teazle at the base are taken from the Cloth-workers' arms. The teazle is a thistle head, used to raise the nap on woollen cloth. The ermine chevron is also a reference to Bishop Ken, who was buried at St John's Church in 1711. The gold chevron is derived from the Leversedge arms. Above the chevron are two sallow trees (willows), a reference to the forest of Selwood or 'Sallow Wood' – a hunting forest in Saxon and Norman times.

The Crest above the shield is a helm (helmet) with a closed visor and mantling in sable and gold. The closed helm signifies that the arms belong to a corporation rather than an individual. On top

of the helm is a gold Saxon crown, a reference to Frome's connection with two Saxon kings: King Athelstan held a witan or assembly at Frome in 934 and King Eadred died here in 955.

The dragon gules (red dragon) rising from the crown is the Wessex Dragon which also appears on the arms of Somerset. It supports a gold crozier (shepherd's crook), a reference to the Abbey of Cirencester, to which the church of St. John's was granted in 1133.

The motto below the shield 'Time Trieth Troth' is from the Hungerford family, major local landowners in the fifteenth and sixteenth centuries. It can be rendered as 'Time will tell how trustworthy you are'.

The arms were designed by H Ellis Tomlinson, who also designed the arms of Bridgwater, Crewkerne and Bathavon.